GRINDHAUS

Grindhaus

The Haus Arrest Anthology

original columns by

MICHAEL SERINGHAUS

YTR
PRESS

New Haven

Publisher: Michael Seringhaus / YTR Press.
Cover design: Michael Seringhaus.

    www.seringhaus.net

These columns originally appeared in the *Yale Daily News*, Yale University, New Haven, CT.

ISBN: 978-0-615-25456-2

For WFB

CONTENTS

POP CULTURE

THE ASTRONAUT AND THE DIAPER: A SORDID TALE

FEBRUARY 8, 2007

W hat do NASA astronauts do between missions? Until this week, I might have guessed modestly: training, book work, perhaps some checkers. Seedy love triangles and diaper-clad interstate crime sprees were fairly near the bottom of the list.

No more.

On Monday, astronaut Lisa Marie Nowak was arrested at the Orlando airport and charged with attempted kidnapping. Supposedly Nowak, who is married with three children, was enmeshed in a romantic struggle with space shuttle pilot William Oefelein and another NASA employee. Nowak apparently sought to confront this third party, Air Force Capt. Colleen Shipman, to discuss their competing relationships with the pilot. She accomplished this by driving 900 miles from Houston to Orlando — wearing a diaper so as to avoid rest stops — before donning a wig and trench coat to assault Ms. Shipman with pepper spray in a parking lot. That move earned her the kidnapping arrest, although when police found the air pistol, buck knife, latex gloves, rubber tubing and garbage bags Nowak had brought along, the charge was upped to attempted murder in the first degree. That's no laughing matter.

The diaper, though, is.

In all my years of film-going, story-reading and news-scouring, I've never before come across an outlaw so intent on the swift commission of crime as to actually don a diaper. Astronauts are taught by NASA to put mission first, ahead of personal concerns or a swollen bladder. Armed with this training, Lisa Nowak has rocketed around the planet, spacewalked for hours, and now soiled herself on Interstate 10.

It turns out that astronauts regularly wear diapers during three phases of spaceflight: liftoff, re-entry and spacewalks. Called Maximum Absorption Garments (MAG), these high-tech potty-pants are special: They are larger than normal adult diapers and, according to NASA, considerably more advanced.

Disposable diapers represent a $22 billion industry worldwide; for decades, manufacturers have touted their latest commercial diaper as revolutionary in both absorbance and comfort. Is it possible that NASA quietly trumped them all, and for years has been quite literally sitting on the future of incontinence protection? What is this space-age wicking material for galaxy-sized messes? A million full-bellied toddlers need to know.

Despite some hearty Google searching, I could find no solid technical information on the NASA diaper. Sure, the National Space Biomedical Research Institute raves that the MAG "is the finest and most absorbent diaper ever made," but that's standard bluster. Nowhere could I find key information such as the intended age range or price per nappy, nor did I determine whether babies wearing NASA brand spontaneously sob. More damning still, there was no mention of the volume of blue liquid a single MAG can absorb — the globally accepted standard for assessing diapers, as any television viewer knows.

It's easy to claim that a product is "more advanced" — but respect in the diaper business is earned, not given. The MAG may be a legendary space garment, but for all we know it could perform on par with a Kleenex thong, or a wad of rock moss stuffed into some jockey shorts. For anyone to take the MAG seriously, NASA needs to pony up some real info, and fast.

If you think waterproof undies are only for old folks, babies and space travel, prepare for a change. Advanced technology from space missions has a way of filtering down to society at large. Like powdered ice cream or the waterproof space pen, adult diaper use may soon go mainstream.

Consider the benefits. Wearing a diaper by choice lends immediate urgency to any endeavor, signaling those around you that you are most certainly in a hurry. Organize your CD collection in traditional underwear and you risk being disturbed or called away; but organize those same CDs wearing a diaper and you're sure to be left in peace. Tired of co-workers interrupting you as you type that report? Try a diaper, and savor the silence. The willingness to eschew bathroom breaks is a powerful statement, adding a certain gravitas to your day. Plus, in winter, your pants are self-heating.

We know Capt. Nowak meant business: In her cross-country drive to confront her rival, she used space-tested waste-management techniques to beat the clock. One does wonder whether she wore the familiar NASA-issue MAG or chose the more affordable and accessible Depend(R) brand Belted Shields. After all, once she surpassed that psychological hurdle and was willing to soil her knickers en route to a felony kidnapping, the least she could do was spare taxpayers the bill.

This story is already fueling countless droll headlines across the country. Understandably so: It's not every day that the Orange Suits get busted playing Dangerous Liaisons at Johnson Space Center or a wayward rocket-jockey spends the night in the graybar hotel. This was one small drive for her man … one giant stretch of hard time. Houston, she has a problem.

Seriously though, a love-struck astronaut did just drive 900 miles in a diaper. You know what they say: If you want to be a comedian these days, just tell people what really happened.

'SNAKES' COULDN'T BITE AFTER TOO MUCH HYPE

SEPTEMBER 1, 2006

T he big Hollywood story this week is the underperformance of New Line Cinema's "Snakes on a Plane." After months of wild Internet hoopla, the kitschy thriller starring cult icon Samuel L. Jackson opened to a dismal $15.4 million -- far below even the most pessimistic estimates.

Was the film itself to blame? I went to North Haven to find out.

I plopped down in an empty cinema, munching Gummi Snakes and ready to pan this fantastic flop. My verdict? "Snakes on a Plane" is a B-movie creature film, retrofit with extra dialogue and camped up to sate its swollen Internet fan base. It's bad, but not spectacularly so. I can't imagine that anyone expected very much more, and as such the film delivers almost exactly what it promised: fun, cheesy action with a ludicrous premise and some slumming stars.

A not-bad movie tailor-made for its rabid, frenzied fans? In these days of empty brand image where any steak can sizzle, "SoaP" should have been a slam dunk. So what crashed this astronomical hype machine?

The Web is abuzz with theories: the hype peaked too soon; the R rating excluded a large chunk of its target audience; the film took itself too seriously; the public took it too seriously, thereby missing its camp appeal and refusing to see it; cult classics never make money at the box office; and so on. To an extent, all are probably true. But the main reason, I think, is different: You can't dupe the Internet jokesters.

In the world of big business, Internet culture is not well understood. Sure, studios may commission glitzy websites and buy online ads, but the whole blog, chat and discussion board culture is foreign to them. This leaves studio execs in a bit of a pickle: They're keen to harness grassroots Internet buzz -- look what it did for "The Blair Witch Project" -- but never quite sure how to do it.

In this, studios should be careful what they wish for. "Snakes on a Plane" was perhaps Hollywood's best attempt yet to spark Internet buzz and achieve pre-release cult status. And as such, it succeeded beautifully.

I first heard about "SoaP" on a discussion board this spring, by which time the spoofing was already well underway. Like any good Internet meme, the concept was a highly efficient replicator, the story being "Can you believe it? They're actually making this!" The campy concept -- as simple as the title, really -- lent itself to interpretation and exploitation through cartoons, T-shirt designs, videos and songs. Net users delighted in hastily-crafted mash-ups and Photoshop-fueled satire. Another inside joke roared around the Internet, and a good laugh was had by all.

This all sounds like good publicity, and without question, it was. So why didn't it translate to actual box office performance? Hollywood wants answers.

The immediate temptation is to dismiss Internet culture as unimportant. After all, the memesphere seized upon this film and hyped it almost beyond belief, but those darn bloggers couldn't fill theatres -- and worse, their machinations didn't sway the movie-going public. Ergo, the Internet is full of geeks whose perverse brand of grassroots spoof-worship isn't worth the price of a pop-up.

But Internet culture isn't geared toward boosting box office revenues. Quite the reverse; this is a culture that prizes free access to entertainment, legal or otherwise, the same culture that embraced Napster, YouTube and BitTorrent. People will spend all day surfing "free tour" porn sites, but paying subscribers are few. Online retailers complain of "phantom shoppers" abandoning loaded carts at the payment screen. The popular iTunes Music Store is widely used to preview songs, but those worth owning are sought on peer-to-peer file sharing systems. The attentions of the Internet crowd are famously fickle, and mysteriously vanish when you actually force a sale.

New Line Cinema courted the hype and forecast a home run. They figured people would shell out $10 for the culmination of the one-line running gag they'd harped upon all summer. In so doing, they fell for the oldest trap of online marketing: equating traffic with actual revenue.

In all, "Snakes on a Plane" did about as well as "Final Destination 3" and "The Hills Have Eyes" -- similar movies with virtually no pre-release publicity. Of course, "SoaP" has done something those other films will never do: It has achieved broad cultural recognition, and entered the hall of fame of Internet memes -- right alongside "All Your Base" and the Star Wars Kid. It's a grand and beloved inside joke for countless Web users. Unfortunately for Hollywood, you just can't put a price on that.

There is perhaps a lesson to be taken from all this, particularly with so many bright-eyed, bushy-tailed Yalies starting school this week. The Ivy League is unquestionably hyped in its own way, idol-ized by high schoolers as a gateway to happiness, riches or whatever. There is a temptation to attach unrealistic expectations to this, to coast on the name. But the brand will only carry you so far. Devote yourself to fashioning a great product, and you can do anything you choose.

After all, no one likes empty hype.

THE BITTERSWEET MELODY OF RACIST TUNES

OCTOBER 27, 2005

This past weekend, a friend pointed me in the direction of a wholly repugnant new music phenomenon. Here's the pitch: Picture twin 13-year-old California-bred blondes with gleaming braces clogging their cutesy smiles. Picture these adorable twins strumming three-quarters-size guitars, wailing rock ballads from a makeshift stage plucked from any small heartland county fair. Oh, and picture them wearing Hitler T-shirts while rocking out about white supremacy.

Meet Prussian Blue. The girls, Lynx and Lamb Gaede -- who look barely old enough to play Mario Kart, let alone "awaken their race" -- have their own Web site and are releasing their second CD. They perform mainly covers of existing white supremacist music, though they are adding some ditties of their own. Their site features a photo gallery, primarily offering snaps of the duo sporting dirndls and relaxing on grassy hillocks, or playing with their infant sister, Dresden.

At first glance, it's unclear what's most appalling: the blithe innocence of these cheery-faced younglings as they proclaim Aryan superiority, or their obvious early soaking in racial intolerance and bigotry, which smacks of child exploitation. We'd like to believe that sweet young things like the Gaede sisters are incapable of spontaneously generating thoughts of racial cleansing, and sure enough, the twins are the daughters of April Gaede, a writer for the white-power publication National Vanguard. Clearly, the girls are a sculpted ploy, the latest and most vile cry for attention from the tiny minority of Nazi-obsessed skinhead idiots on the ultraconservative right. As such, they are easily dismissed.

Or are they? The girls of Prussian Blue were the subject of an "ABC PrimeTime" report last week. Blogs everywhere have picked them up, and decidedly non-racist people are now puzzling over their work. They have transcended the ambit of their political birthplace. This growing cultural penetration is worrisome.

I offer here a brief review of Prussian Blue, to spare the inquisitive among you the unpleasant experience I just endured -- namely, that of rummaging through ultranationalist sectarianism to satisfy my curiosity about these underage sirens of race-hate.

Prussian Blue's album "Fragment of a Future" was released by Resistance Records, but their song "I Will Bleed for You" can be heard for free online. I did myself the unpardonable disservice of listening to this, to better gauge the musical and lyrical talents of Lynx and Lamb.

Quite simply, the music is rubbish. Honestly, it's safe to assume that these tonally-challenged girls would be playing to an audience of catatonic family members in their basement if it weren't for the outrageous slant of their message. While kid groups with real talent do come and go, Prussian Blue is decidedly not among them. The music is unsophisticated, clumsy and unpleasant, and any endearing quality in their unschooled voices is extinguished by the abrasive content of their lyrics. You'll find better arranged tracks on a Wesley Willis album.

Granted, ABC isn't profiling Prussian Blue for their melodic mastery. We care about their lyrics.

World-weary middle-schoolers Lynx and Lamb bemoan the rape of our land and admonish citizens for idly "watching as the white flame dies." While unquestionably replete with arrogant posturing, the song itself isn't particularly angry. In fact, for a white-supremacy group, Prussian Blue is downright tepid, offering mostly muddled symbolism and vague calls to action. The lyrics are a confusing and superficial gloss of the white supremacist position, and first-time listeners will understandably wonder what these two are crooning about. This dangerously clever play means Prussian Blue serves as a gateway drug, preparing youngsters for stronger material later on. (For the curious, Max Resist, a rock group sharing the Resistance Records label, offers such charming lyrics as "let the cities burn / let the streets run red / if you ain't White / you'll be dead.")

Listening to these schoolgirls, it's tempting to overlook the fact that the racist hate they espouse is very real. For instance, they sent aid specifically earmarked for white victims of Hurricane Katrina. (ABC reports that these donations were largely rejected when would-be recipients learned the identity of the senders.) Their grandfather has registered the swastika as his cattle-brand. They are also Holocaust deniers. When interviewed about the band's name by Viceland magazine, Lynx and Lamb replied, "Prussian Blue is just a really pretty color. There is also the discussion of the lack of 'Prussian Blue' coloring (Zyklon-B residue) in the so-called gas chambers in the concentration camps. We think it might make people question some of the inaccuracies of the 'Holocaust' myth." With crowd-pleasing replies like that one, I don't think Britney Spears need fear for her seat anytime soon.

Prussian Blue's trump card is confusion: beaming pre-teen girls touting eugenics and bigotry. The conflation of imagery is jarring. But Lynx and Lamb are neither cute nor benign, and their apparent innocence does not sanitize their message. They are a mouthpiece for racists, bigots and white supremacists, a sad reminder that civilized society must remain vigilant. While mass adoption of their views is unthinkable, the real danger is that Prussian Blue will continue to turn heads, and hoodwink their way into the public eye. Hatred must remain appalling, however watered-down, prettied-up or sweet-smiling it may appear.

NBC's 'Three Wishes' is a Parade of Embarassing Consumerism

November 10, 2005

E very now and then, something comes along that makes me question the fundamental tenets of consumer society. The most recent catalyst: a new show on NBC called "Three Wishes."

The program teams washed-up Christian crooner Amy Grant with a squad of peppy co-hosts. Together, they rain joy on the deserving hordes. But this sly show is more than a feel-good tear-jerker; it is the cancerous outgrowth of a culture obsessed with material consumption.

The basic concept of "Three Wishes" is noble enough, if oddly misguided: Grant and her band of merry men travel the country, ferreting out deserving folks. Then, these model citizens have their wishes granted. Conveniently, they often wish for consumer goods, which means the show is basically an hour-long product placement as wish after wish is granted, propelling the recipients into tear-streaming convulsions of glee. Shot though soft filter and well-stocked with weeping mothers, the show is a curious half-breed: It marries the maudlin potency of a TV movie with all the cultish consumerist jingoism of an Amway pep rally. The result is like Judgment Day for small-time Samaritans, if the cosmic reward for wholesome living were a new kitchen from Home Depot.

One week, Ameriquest Mortgage gave McMansions to Iraq veterans. Then Jeep gave two young men new Commanders with moonroofs and seven-passenger seating. One recent episode featured Tim, a small-town California sheriff and step-father of an adorable and selfless little boy. This boy's only wish was to give something back to Tim for being such a terrific step-dad. Tim once drove a gigantic Ford F-350 pickup, but had to surrender it for financial reasons. Thankfully Grant was on hand to set this right, because such injustice simply cannot stand.

Swayed by the touching story -- and not at all by the hour of prime-time network exposure -- Ford Motor Company sent two gifts: a brand new F-350, and a smarmy PR man to glad-hand the cop, grin to America and hand over the keys. Tim cheered and wept. A local authority figure reduced to sycophancy for a 10-mpg monstrosity: truly, an American dream come true.

But for all its schmaltzy sentimentality, "Three Wishes" is built on solid consumerist assumptions. It never crossed the producers' minds that Sheriff Tim might actually have done the right thing selling his pickup, that the insurance or fuel costs were excessive or that the vehicle was an extravagance. It never occurred to them that 20-year-old soldiers fresh from service might actually be better off living in their $400-per-month basement than some lavish new house with five-digit property taxes. The unspoken assumption is that more is better, that every citizen deserves a 4,000-sq. foot Beltway Baronial with cathedral ceilings and trappings of the good life. "Three Wishes" faithfully mirrors the national fascination with living large.

Over-consumption is epidemic. While families have shrunk, the average size of single-family houses has soared from 963-sq. feet in 1950 to nearly 2,400-sq. feet today. The average American household carries $9,000 in credit card debt, and the national savings rate just dipped below zero. Five years of cheap money has spurred borrowing at incredible levels, fueling a speculative bubble in real estate and coaxing citizens to indulge every material craving with borrowed funds. Proportional spending has increased significantly, along with debt. We mortgage tomorrow to live well today.

Fueling this frenzy is a distortion: many people have a wholly unrealistic view of how the typical American lives. Supposedly middleclass sitcom families are depicted in upper-class living spaces. "Three Wishes" informs us that good fathers "deserve" pricey pickups. Virtually everyone on TV is happy, well-dressed and consuming at a high level.

Marketing is so forceful that we can no longer distinguish between needs and wants. Watch enough television, and you'll feel positively poor without two plasma TVs or a three-car garage.

The almighty consumer has become pretender king. He operates not in his own material self interest, but, like some runaway engine of gratification, consumes in overdrive to satisfy manufactured wants not his own.

This insatiable hunger is driven by contemporary marketing campaigns that border on the absurd: a woman has racy dreams, moaning as she shops for coats; mothers "ooh" and "ahh" over J.C. Penney coupons; and, my personal favorite, Circuit City urges us to buy flat-panel TVs for every room. Advertisements this preposterous risk breaking our trance, laying bare the unquenchable and ongoing orgy that pairs unwitting citizens with crap they don't need.

It's time to put some reason back into laissez-faire capitalism. With the debauchery of holiday season fast approaching, it is especially challenging to combat the allure of needless consumption. Amy Grant says we deserve a big house and a pickup. I say we deserve to be financially solvent and free of junk.

Take your pick, and be careful what you wish for.

On TV's 'Loser,' the unlikely happens

December 1, 2005

Thanks to NBC's "Biggest Loser," weight loss has became a spectator sport. The season two finale aired Tuesday, occupying two hours of prime airtime. This program has been a runaway success, presumably finding a ready audience in the countless Americans who funnel billions of dollars annually into the diet industry.

It has been suggested that the 25 percent of Americans who are obese face discrimination that is subtle and widespread. The self-defeating nature of the diet business contributes to feelings of hopelessness among those seeking to lose weight, and against this backdrop, NBC's "Biggest Loser" is -- dare I say it -- surprisingly refreshing.

Like many others, I am generally suspicious of businesses selling weight-loss techniques. Because such ventures depend upon overweight people to fuel profits, they face a not-so-subtle conflict of interest: Any technique that legitimately helps people drop pounds in a sustainable manner will cannibalize its own client base in quite short order. Selling diets is an awfully short-lived business if the product actually works.

Granted, it is hardly challenging to criticize "Biggest Loser." After all, this is a show that takes morbidly obese Americans, crams them into spandex, then films them groaning through workouts and panting their way up shallow hills. Millions tune in to watch fat people struggle, weep, burst their Lycra and squabble for money. If life in America is a game of status-display one-upsmanship, and the fat are the silent underclass, then "Biggest Loser" is schadenfreude at its absolute finest.

No discussion of this series would be complete without at least a cursory look at some of the more absurd fallacies it presents. Consider, for instance, the notion that to effectively weigh fat people you need a scale the size of a vehicle, complete with flat-panel LCD monitors. Or that, to increase user suspense, these precision instruments deliberately display a series of incorrect values for several seconds before revealing the true measurement. (NBC should market such scales to scientists, who might welcome such excitement at the weigh station.) Perhaps worst of all is the subtle overstatement of the rewards of slimming down. For most people, losing 50 pounds is a remarkable and health-enhancing achievement, but doing so does not conjure $100,000 into your checking account or draw everyone you've met from middle school onward to stand cheering on your driveway.

But the simple fact is that the contestants on this program lost a truly astonishing amount of weight. Finalists Seth, Suzy and winner Matt went from bulbous heavyweights to razor-thin, cut-and-pumped hotties right before our eyes. Admittedly, they were chasing a quarter of a million dollars under the constant harassment of personal trainers and with TV cameras thrust in their faces. Say what you will; they're all now amazingly thin.

Against all odds -- despite the teary eliminations, the manufactured drama, the hammed-up emotion and relentless product placement -- "Biggest Loser" was fascinating, for the simple reason that it showed in plain view the astounding elasticity of the human body.

Of course, this doesn't concern NBC in the slightest. But ratings most certainly do, and this week's finale garnered the network a home run Tuesday night, beating the rest of the competition by a wide margin. As a result, NBC is already hard at work casting season three, and plans to launch a spin-off series in early 2006. And true to form, they are profiteering at a giddy pace, releasing the "Biggest Loser Workout" DVD and book (featuring cast members) this holiday season. They have even gone so far as to milk money from their audience, launching an online pay-as-you-go support group for those hoping to mimic the success of the contestants.

Still, the national fascination with obesity is not translating to actual slimming. Last month, news wires carried a story about a supposed revolt against the health craze in America, with fast food chains unveiling newer, fattier meals and posting record profits nationwide. Indeed, I wonder how long "Biggest Loser" itself can persist, with its opening credits touting the need for willpower in the face of temptation. Here NBC producers should be careful what they wish for, since a sudden bout of self-discipline might cause audiences not only to lose weight, but to halt their frenzied consumption of products pushed by the network's advertisers.

"Biggest Loser" is sure to ignite debate, and the show's many humorous aspects definitely invite a roast. But these should not obscure the fact that the transformations achieved by the top contestants through eight months of diet and exercise are nothing short of remarkable. And if this causes just one person to abandon that exhausting and costly cocktail of self-propagating literature, weight-loss groups and overpriced diet aids, the show will have served an unexpected and valuable purpose.

PLUCKY VILLAINS GLAMORIZED IN MOVIES, REALITY

MARCH 2, 2006

I t's the type of story usually confined to the silver screen: a gang of expert thieves, employing a host of techniques from police impersonation to so-called "tiger kidnapping," robbed a plain-looking cash depot in Tonbridge, England last week and made off with 53 million pounds ($93 million). The largest cash robbery in a nation known for them, this was a heist worthy of Hollywood. That fact is stirring interesting ripples in public opinion.

The thieves' strategy could pass for reel two of a big-budget thriller. In a highly coordinated attack, two members of the gang driving a mocked-up police car pulled over depot manager Colin Dixon during his drive home. He was handcuffed, and driven off in the phony cruiser as two spurious constables lured the manager's wife and young son from their home. His family bound and threatened at gunpoint in a remote location, the manager was forced to open the depot and watch as millions in banknotes rumbled off in a large white truck. Neither the manager nor his family was ultimately harmed, and the thieves -- so far, at least -- appear to have made off in safety.

The criminals' apparent I.Q. soared further in the days following the raid, when police recovered a van laden with 15 million pounds in uncirculated, sequentially-numbered banknotes. It takes a cool-headed thief indeed to jettison $26 million in hard cash simply because the bills might prove traceable. The work of amateurs this was not.

Smart thieves, no casualties, a massive haul -- the story seems strangely familiar, and with good reason. We're well-accustomed to sly robbers outwitting on-screen cops. For decades, Hollywood has pumped our communal unconscious full of good-natured rogues and their daring capers. Alarms have been bypassed, safes drilled and jewels snatched as we munch buttered popcorn in the dark.

It is interesting to note that our collective experience cheering celluloid thieves seemingly carries over into real life. The British authorities are battling a strong social countercurrent in chasing down the crooks, because a surprising fraction of the public actually seems to be cheering them on.

The U.K. boasts a rich history of massive heists -- from the Great Train Robbery of 1963 ($56 million in today's currency), to the 1983 Brinks-Mat robbery at Heathrow Airport ($45 million in bullion and diamonds) and the IRA-executed Northern Bank job in Belfast in 2004 ($45 million in cash) -- and more to the point, an equally long history of glamorizing the criminals who perpetrate them. In films and stories alike, the mythology of the master thief is entrenched.

And so, public outrage at the Tonbridge theft is tempered by a sneaking, guilty admiration for its perpetrators. One commentator dubbed the heist an "El Dorado" -- the kind of score a master thief can retire on. A former bank robber appeared on the BBC's "Newsnight" program, praising the crime and expressing his hope that at

least some of the men get away with it. The Independent, a daily newspaper, even published a helpful addendum entitled "How to Launder
50 Million Pounds," which offered expert advice to would-be thieves
-- and, no doubt, to the real ones. With national newspapers dispens-
ing money-laundering tips to crooks on the lam, it's tough to fault
the public for lending mere moral support. Somewhere, a thief is
smiling. And he probably looks a lot like DeNiro.

Yet one senses the displeasure of the powers that be, as if the
public, like a mischievous child caught thrashing in his mashed po-
tatoes, has again found entertainment in the wrong place. Lionizing
gun-toting crooks in the midst of a manhunt simply will not do. Last
week, the dour nannies of Britain's op-ed pages ran somber com-
mentaries reminding us that, in essence, life is not Hollywood, these
crooks are not George Clooney and we should all be ashamed of
ourselves.

They are, of course, correct. Dixon and his family endured a
frightful ordeal, and violent crime is not something to celebrate.

Still, it's not hard to see why people secretly sympathize with the
baddies. The very same week as the Tonbridge heist, a new Harrison
Ford film opened, called "Firewall." It details a plot to kidnap a bank
security manager and hold his family for ransom to expedite a massive theft. Sound familiar?

Giddy disbelief accompanies life imitating art in this manner, as
though the real world owes us a duty to be far more boring and
predictable than any Hollywood script. But fantasy and reality are
intertwined, each influencing the other. After all, "Top Gun" resulted
in a massive upsurge in real-world Navy applications, and "CSI" has
transformed the once dull forensics field into a magnet for school
kids. One has to wonder if the Tonbridge gang didn't take a certain
pleasure in aping their own film-driven lore, in living up to the myths.

No doubt, their own exploits will soon be immortalized in film.

The Tonbridge raid was real. No credits will roll, and I don't envy the crooks -- who, cunning as they may be, still face a lifetime of looking over their shoulders. Perhaps our sympathies should remain with our on-screen heroes, whose getaways are always clean, and whose wry smiles betray hearts of gold.

Show's vision of justice seems, well, perverted

MARCH 8, 2007

On Tuesday, Dateline NBC aired the latest in what has become an ongoing series of Internet crime reports titled "To Catch a Predator." Hosted by Chris Hansen and employing the smut-talking prowess of volunteers from civilian group Perverted Justice, the series ensnares would-be sex offenders and exposes them on national television. But during its growing number of installments, this increasingly sensationalist program has worn out its welcome. Its problems are too serious to ignore.

The premise is straightforward. Volunteers from Perverted Justice pose as underage Internet users and hang around popular chat rooms. When hit up for chat, they freely wander into explicit territory, swap photos and lure their target to a real-life meeting. The unwitting mark arrives to find himself pinned both by hidden cameras and Chris Hansen's local-affiliate swagger; this terrifying one-two punch sends the "predator" staggering into the sunlight, at which point he is thrown to the ground and arrested by porky local sheriffs wearing tactical vests. The result is a curious cross between Candid Camera and COPS, with some Sunday-morning proselytizing thrown in.

It is tempting to dismiss the show as televised entrapment. Addressing this issue on the Dateline blog, NBC anchor Stone Phillips '77 admits that "in many cases, the decoy is the first to bring up the subject of sex." He goes on to assert that "once the hook is baited, the fish jump and run with it like you wouldn't believe." This does little to excuse the underlying charge: Do Perverted Justice decoys entice men to type things they otherwise would not? It's impossible to know for certain — but provided it fuels more episodes, Dateline doesn't seem to mind.

The stings depend upon the efforts of Perverted Justice, the civilian group that specializes in aping minors online. It seems such work would demand of volunteers a certain clinical detachment; though they may mimic capricious, uneducated 'tweens on Instant Messenger, in reality — one hopes — they are anything but.

I visited Perverted-Justice.com to find out. I was dismayed to find sandbox rhetoric and perhaps the most petulant FAQ section online today. Click the question "How is this a crime? There was no actual minor!" and you are treated to a meandering hypothetical response, which begins: "Such a stupid statement. If you're reading this and you've uttered this at any point of your life, feel free to smack yourself for ignorance right now." They also caution that they're very powerful and well connected, and that "threatening us is a very, very bad idea."

Interestingly, Dateline busts are just a fraction of the group's activities. Their main trade appears to be independent baiting expeditions in chat rooms followed by extensive online information gathering and "outing" of targets on the Web. This might include posting the street address, telephone number and other details about a mark in an online forum. Such information could then be used to humiliate and harass the individual and their family.

One might argue that pedophiles and "predators" deserve such punishment, but even so it is hardly the place of pseudonym-sporting civilians to dole it out.

Any group entrusted with assisting criminal investigations should be professional, accountable and free of amateurish posturing. Perverted Justice would do best to confine its efforts to supporting law enforcement, not striking out alone to lynch citizens without due process. One certainly hopes their volunteers are driven by genuine concern for children, not the giddy rush of power that accompanies the public "outing" of Web users.

The group also highlights its rate of return. "Riverside, California: 51 predators in three days. Darke County, Ohio: Completely rural, two hours from anything ... 17 predators in three days."

I'd like to see evidence that Perverted Justice excludes false positives: Once caught in a chat with a decoy, does anyone escape being branded a "predator?" I could find no chat log or statistic reporting this outcome, although the "Info for Police" page does mention a "100 percent conviction rate."

Frankly, I'm reluctant to accept that Internet-savvy pedophiles are as utterly ubiquitous as Perverted Justice would have us believe. If they are not, care should be taken in our efforts to snare them; most users online are still innocent bystanders. Teen chat rooms are not sanitized by populating them with garrulous, lewd-minded decoys.

Moreover, myriad pitfalls exist. Age is routinely misrepresented online; what if a 24-year-old "predator" turns out to be 17? In that case, the Perverted Justice approach is equivalent to seducing a minor with lascivious chat, or soliciting sexual photos from an underage user. Which network will air that sting?

For now, "To Catch a Predator" continues. We can lament its slide into shock journalism, but a program that catches deviant men seeking to prey upon underage victims does have some claim to a moral high ground. Few criminals are as despised as pedophiles, and the public will tolerate exceptional means of capturing them. Nonetheless, the national news media has obligations beyond sating the raucous mob.

We would like to believe that NBC and its bedfellows are not only doing the right thing, but doing it properly. Online predators are a real problem, but as any preteen knows, two wrongs don't make a right.

DEGENERES' CELEBRITY EMOTIONS HARM PET ADOPTION

OCTOBER 24, 2007

A confession: I'm not quite so immersed in pop culture as my faithful readers may think. Yes, I've written about astronauts in diapers, SpongeBob SquarePants and ninja burglars — but in truth, I'm really not hip.

The fact is, my friends have spotted my willingness to fuel biweekly opinion pieces with tabloid fodder and now interpret this as an open invitation to send me the latest Hollywood gossip as column ideas. Some of these are dead ends — there's only so much to be said about Britney's deteriorating physique — but once in a while these stories merit a closer look. Just such a thing happened last week, when daytime television host Ellen Degeneres erupted in tears on air, bemoaning the plight of her adopted dog Iggy.

The facts are straightforward. Ellen apparently adopted Iggy (described as a "Brussels-Griffon mix") from the Mutts and Moms pet adoption agency in Pasadena. When her cats refused to tolerate the animal, Ellen gave the dog to her hairdresser and her two children. Iggy had already bonded with the loving kids when the adoption agency learned of the owner switch. Ellen's handoff was a violation of their contract, so the agency reclaimed the mutt.

Iggy's seizure prompted Ellen to bawl on air for several minutes, which in turn spawned a tempest of secondary media attention. Enraged citizens sprang to action — after all, any group that could turn the normally genial Degeneres into a sniffling wreck on national television must surely be the devil incarnate — and demanded the dog be returned to the hairdresser.

The agency has thus far stood fast, and rightly so.

Ignoring for a moment the star power of the sobbing provocateur, the agency in this instance faces what is likely a routine problem in their business. It's tough to vilify organizations that place abandoned or rescued animals into caring homes. These operations are generally volunteer-run, not-for-profit businesses that take careful precautions to ensure that their animals, many of which have been abused in past, do not endure hardship again. Adoptive families are screened, and agreements drafted, in the animals' interests.

These volunteers work daily to match abused or rejected creatures with honest owners, and they do so without demanding public recognition or coverage on daytime talk programs. It is disappointing that their first such attention came in the form of a maudlin j'accuse by a petulant TV star — one who didn't bother to read her contract, created a no-win situation and punished the agency for her mistake.

Even Ellen agrees she is responsible for this mess. But that said, isn't it unjust to snatch poor Iggy from his newfound family?

Yes and no.

Begin law school, and you will likely find that seemingly elemental concepts like justice can prove maddeningly difficult to pin down.

For starters, there are at least two approaches to administering justice in any individual dispute: a backward-looking view which decides what is fair for the parties concerned, and a forward-looking approach which creates incentives for future just behavior.

Let's say the hairdresser's family would indeed make a good home for Iggy — that they would have passed the agency's screening tests, had they thought to apply. To do justice in the backward-looking sense, then, the unfortunate dog should be returned to the family posthaste. Pet abduction never did sit well with prepubescent kids, and there is no reason to deny them an animal they're qualified to adopt.

But justice ex ante is quite different. Allowing adopters to redistribute animals at their discretion would trivialize the screening process. We don't deal with human adoptions in this way, and presumably those who care deeply enough about animals to volunteer their time rescuing them might think them equally precious. As Atlanta Falcons quarterback Michael Vick recently reminded us, people want dogs for many reasons indeed; those unable to adopt an animal themselves may attempt to do so through a friend. Adoption agencies screen for a reason, and their efforts to secure kind homes for pets should not be circumvented by awarding full discretion to well-meaning but ill-experienced foster owners.

To decide Iggy's fate, then, which approach is correct? Does one family's well-publicized trauma outweigh our desire to see animals reliably cared for in future?

Ellen herself clearly favors corrective justice, the backward-looking or ex post approach. In this, she is like most parties involved in dispute. Normal people seek a fair resolution to their own particular problems; few are so selfless as to sacrifice their interests to achieve a more robust system of societal incentive.

But Ellen is not a normal person. She commands an audience of millions, and her performance last week reached far beyond her usual demographic. Instead of offering a fair treatment of the issues at stake, she knowingly begged a groundswell of heartland sympathy — and in so doing, encouraged a tragic, public condemnation of a well-intentioned, underfunded and much-needed charity. She should be ashamed.

Mutts and Moms deserves our praise. By refusing to play favorites, they remind us that some people take their jobs seriously.

If only Ellen would do the same.

THE BACHELOR'S BRAD EXPOSES REAL REALITY LOVE

NOVEMBER 28, 2007

L ast Monday, the 11th installment of ABC's The Bachelor came to an unexpected and riveting conclusion: After whittling the field from 25 nubile women to his final two, Brad Womack — the rugged Texan bar-owner and self-made millionaire — dumped them both. In his break with tradition, the Southern beau laid bare the folly of this preposterous program.

The following day, ABC aired "The Bachelor: After the Final Rose," wherein the snubbed ladies returned to face the man who sent them home. Though such piggyback specials are typical — a way to squeeze another night's ratings out of the finale — this one was unusually awkward. Judging by the booing, grimacing and head-shaking in the studio audience, Brad's choice was unpopular indeed.

It's easy to see why viewers feel violated: Brad broke the rules. At its core, The Bachelor is implicitly a contract. We the public anoint one man, and give him a stable of beauties from which to select his mate. In return, we demand to be entertained: he shall slowly pare the field down to one, and there shall be True Love. Nothing shall interfere with this hallowed process, and in no event shall he be so ungrateful and so arrogant as to look beyond his women.

In other words, rejecting 24 ladies means love; rejecting 25 is a drink in the face of a benevolent public and an affront to romance in general.

For a series that matches dozens of beautiful, pre-screened women with one successful and ostensibly desirable man, the show has a remarkably poor track record in fostering real relationships. Of the 10 previous Bachelor installments, all but two unions have ended in breakup and only one has yielded a lasting engagement. The franchise's lone and oft-touted success, the televised marriage of Trista and Ryan Sutter, is in fact drawn from the companion series The Bachelorette, which turns the tables and puts a single woman among two dozen men.

It's no wonder the show rarely succeeds. It is unlikely that any one group of 25 women — even when screened for age, looks and relationship status — will include a given man's future wife. People are too picky; marriage sets the bar too high. Even if by a fluke a good match is formed, the swift early eliminations — 10 girls are sent home on the first night alone — make short work of the pack. Very early on, the bachelor is forced to choose one of only a handful of women, with no credible guarantee that any were right for him in the first place.

This is not to say it's impossible to find one perfect match in 25. But we should not expect to see this outcome with any substantial frequency. The problems don't end there: if two people on the show truly are destined to marry, they might gravitate to one another very quickly — effectively excluding others from the game. Since this would make for boring television, the bachelor is compelled to avoid playing favorites and to date several girls at once — a dilution that, if he were truly smitten by one, might well prove repugnant.

In the end, the series is a corruption of the dating process: a saccharine but soulless love virus that hijacks the hearts of a few dozen people, jerks them around for six weeks and spits them out, single and abused.

One might expect a show so hopeless to flounder, but somehow it's stayed afloat. Viewers rush to the trough year after year to watch artificial romance unfold on screen, choosing to ignore the obvious truth that any relationships thusly born are ersatz facades doomed utterly to failure.

This makes The Bachelor a strange hybrid: "Eternal Sunshine" meets "Mulholland Drive." We know the relationships will fail. No matter: we want to be deceived.

Brad Womack refused to play out our fantasy. He stole our happy ending.

In reality, Brad just remembered what The Bachelor asks us to forget: that love is irrational, bilateral and can't be forced. That the show's history of happy endings is a charade. And that six weeks in a rented mansion dating several women at once is not a good foundation for a relationship. Brad showed America the rats in the kitchen, and with any luck they'll be tough to forget this time.

Of course, the franchise will recover — presumably returning with a new, ironclad contract to ensure one woman is chosen in the end. With this loophole closed, viewers will again be treated to escapist fantasies and insulated from the unpleasant truth about televised romance.

But for now, we can enjoy Brad Womack's legacy. This scruffy rake didn't just reject two pretty girls on national television: he derailed the network's ham-fisted attempts to cram courtship into a prime-time format. He laid bare the perverse truth behind the rose ceremonies, the soft-filter camera work, the ever-cheery bachelor-ettes and the hammy host. For a few short moments, he stripped the whitewash from reality TV.

WITH GREAT POWER AND WEALTH COME ...
'HOT GIRLS'?

MARCH 27, 2008

On the evening of Eliot Spitzer's resignation, a friend of mine — a doctoral candidate in neurophysiology — asked a question point-blank: "So, he got hot girls. Isn't that what rich and powerful guys are supposed to do?"

Despite the question's scoffing delivery, the answer, scientifically at least, is "yes." Wherever hierarchy is found in nature, the most fit individuals traditionally exercise their dominance by commandeering their most desired mates. The precise image of desirability may fluctuate, but the ability of the powerful to acquire it has remained remarkably stable across species and throughout history.

While civilization attempts to filter out such base animal instincts, this one has slipped through the cracks. The right of dominant individuals to the most desirable mates is not just intact, but routinely glorified. Pop culture offers several examples.

ABC's reality show "The Bachelor" returned for its 12th season last week to celebrate, once again, the entitlement of anointed alphas to stay in rented mansions and drive Maseratis while simultaneously dating two dozen women. The show's abysmal record of forging successful relationships suggests that these men are probably just flexing their status muscle before settling down later on. (The clearest evidence of this was offered last season by bachelor Brad Womack, the scruffy Texan who drank the champagne and absorbed the attention before rejecting all the women and leaving the program alone.) Though it is tough to take "The Bachelor" seriously, it does enact in puppet-show form the mate-choice ritual to which successful men are allegedly privy.

After these alphas mature, their next step is Bravo TV's "Millionaire Matchmaker" — a program which answers the call of self-made men with rudimentary social skills who are drunk on one-nighters yet (mysteriously) unfulfilled. In this series, a relationship expert aims to break these wild horses and teach them the virtues of monogamy. In typical fashion, the goal is accomplished by presenting each with a room full of unfailingly beautiful women in cocktail gowns who have all expressed an interest in meeting a man of means. For these privileged men, marriage is merely the final course of the smorgasbord of "The Bachelor."

The same game is rehearsed by countless college kids each spring, when short-lived flings with attractive partners are cast as exercises in confidence-building. Spring break is increasingly a time when students play sex-object — demonstrating their ability to win desirable mates, if only for a single, tequila-fueled night. Term-time book-learning is thus supplemented with the crucial real-world lesson that sex is a strong currency: Go long on hotness and you'll reap tangible rewards.

So those at the top of the chain have their pick of the rest. But my colleague's stark question remains: If society accepts, even endorses, the rights of the fittest to amass desirable partners, then why are we shocked when Eliot Spitzer does precisely that?

Our instinctive reply is that Spitzer is married, and as much as we may glamorize juvenile toe-dipping, mate choice is a one-shot gun. But while many would classify adultery as evidence of moral turpitude, and in many cases rightly so, for public figures the revelation of infidelity is simply another storm to be weathered. Spitzer's successor and his wife both acknowledge straying in the past, evidently to no ill effect; Bill Clinton showed just how raunchy the oval office could get while Hillary slept next door. Whatever adultery may be to a politician, it is certainly not fatal.

The real sticking point is Spitzer's hypocrisy — busting prostitution rings while secretly sampling their wares — and his sullying of a respected public office with illicit criminal activity. This suggests, however, that had he not paid for his trysts Spitzer might still be on the job. In other words, his appetite for seven-diamond women needs no explanation — just paying for them does.

We know where that leaves him. But where does it leave us?

The phenomenon of powerful public officials taking private sexual liberties is unlikely to disappear anytime soon. Paying for sex may be illegal, but buying mates with status is an age-old transaction. Humans will always covet desirable partners, and those in power will often be best situated to get them.

Nonetheless, from a cultural standpoint, glamorizing this basic animal truth seems unnecessary and unhelpful. If we really care about discouraging philandering among our leaders, we should also stop cheering when televised beaus date a dozen models at once. Boycotting "The Bachelor" might not thwart future Spitzers, but when the time comes to condemn their transgressions, at least we won't seem so insincere.

And Yalies take heed, lest we forget Spitzer's academic pedigree. In the ongoing battle between Elihu Yale and John Harvard, this much is clear: Being an Eli still beats being a John.

Borough burglar has 'Real Ultimate Power'

SEPTEMBER 18, 2007

N ews flash: Real Ultimate Power has been unleashed on Staten Island. Yes, the Forgotten Borough has been terrorized by a stealthy burglar dressed like a ninja.

I first heard about this last week. A Yale colleague told me that her parents were awakened by police helicopters with spotlights searching for a ninja who had just robbed the house next door. As a columnist, I will confess: things like this don't happen nearly as often as I would like.

I had to learn more. A ninja? In Staten Island?

Quite so. It seems the ninja first appeared over summer, hitting several ritzy homes in Todt Hill -- the upscale neighborhood that supplied Don Corleone's estate in The Godfather. In over a dozen subsequent burglaries, he -- I assume it is a he -- has knocked over progressively less tony houses, and was most recently spotted stealing an electric guitar from Dongan Hills. Police sketches of the masked suspect are understandably droll.

Apparently this ninja is agile, brazen, and determined. He is reputed to scale walls, enter through skylights or upper-floor windows, and tiptoe about gathering loot. One particularly well-stocked house was so appealing, he burglarized it twice. He carries nunchucks and is not afraid to use them -- a DJ was quite badly bruised when he walked in on the Silent Assassin ganking his DVD player. He is also immune to pain. When said DJ plunged a steak knife into Shinobi's shoulder, the steely-eyed burglar paid no heed. This suggests he is either supernaturally focused, or high as a Georgia pine. (I hope for the former, but fear the latter.)

It is no doubt terrifying to surprise a burglar in your home, and I can only imagine the nightmares I might have after seeing a black-clad stealth warrior skulking around with my home theatre equipment. That said, there is something undeniably comical about this would-be ninja suiting up and prowling about only to be stabbed by a suburban MC with a kitchen knife.

Permit me a brief aside. I once heard of a man who spent years training in ninjutsu, the ninja arts. Inspired by Batman, Chuck Norris or whatever, this fellow earnestly hoped to master the 'way of the shadow' and take his skills to the streets. As (urban) legend holds, when he had mastered the ancient techniques of deadly combat, he dressed in a full ninja outfit, complete with katana, and took a walk through the worst part of Chicago. During this inaugural stroll, a drunken vagrant sprang from an alley and smashed him in the face with a bottle, sending the ninja to critical care and aborting his nascent vigilante career without a single punch thrown. The moral, I think, is subtlety. Even a trained fighter shouldn't call attention to the fact; it only invites trouble.

With this in mind, the Staten Island Ninja has only himself to blame for his knife wound. Would the DJ have stabbed any other robber, or was he driven wild by the sight of a real, actual ninja in his kitchen? Are the nunchucks really sufficient defense, or should he bring throwing stars and smoke bombs next time? And why target Staten Island, anyway? All valid questions the ninja is no doubt pondering in his lair, presumably whilst swapping gauze on his shoulder and hanging upside-down from the rafters.

But the bridge and tunnel night-crawler leaves some questions for us, too. One wonders, for instance, why he started in the fancy neighborhood up the hill, then worked his way slowly to lower ground. Perhaps pawn shops were suspicious of a ninja peddling Harry Winston diamonds -- or perhaps there is simply more demand for electric guitars, religious figurines and family-size bottles of sunless tanner. The black market is fickle.

It is also unclear how he gets away. With no sign of a Batmobile, cargo van or magic carpet idling nearby, it is not apparent how he escapes with electric guitars and other bulky loot. Absent any proof to the contrary, I prefer to imagine the ninja leaping between rooftops under cover of night, stopping to wail hard on his purloined guitar whilst silhouetted against the moon. That would be cool; and by cool, I mean totally sweet.

The ninja as an idea is a cultural icon, cemented by films, video games, and more recently, the Internet. That this imagined history is now being invoked in New York boroughs to pillage suburban chattels is at once fascinating and strangely depressing. One almost hopes a true ninja would travel to Staten Island to stamp out the pretender and restore our faith in the myth. Wishful thinking, of course. True ninjas don't ride the ferry.

In any case, at a school with an overactive police blotter, it is refreshing to remember that some criminals are more funny than threatening.

So as very real crime continues to plague Yale students and New Haven in general, let's tip our hats to the Staten Island Ninja -- for stealing guitars, getting stabbed, and generally putting the smirk back into crime.

SCIENCE & SOCIETY

SCIENTISTS:
CONSIDER WHERE YOU PUBLISH

SEPTEMBER 8, 2004

For scientists, publishing a paper in a respected peer-reviewed journal marks the culmination of successful research. But some of the most prestigious and sought-after journals are so costly to access that a growing number of academic libraries can't afford to subscribe. Before submitting your next manuscript, consider a journal's access policy alongside its prestige - and weigh the implications of publishing in such costly periodicals.

Two distinct problems continue to plague scientific publishing. First, institutional journal subscription costs are skyrocketing so fast that they outstrip the ability of many libraries to pay, threatening to sever scientists from the literature. Second, the taxpaying public funds a terrific amount of research in this country, and with few exceptions, can't access any of it. These problems share a common root: paid access to the scientific literature.

Consider some figures. Subscription fee increases for academic journals have surpassed inflation six-fold throughout the past decade, and the sharpest increases belong to journal titles in medicine and the basic sciences. The Association of Research Libraries examined subscriber spending between 1986 and 2001: by 2001, libraries were spending three times as much for fewer serial titles. With fixed or declining budgets, some academic and institutional libraries can't afford to subscribe to all the journals their scientists demand. Many are cutting acquisitions in the humanities and social sciences to compensate, still unable to keep pace. Scientists are being saddled with a pretty lousy legacy. No wonder the French department hates us.

The dazzling rise in journal subscription costs is logical, considering publishers enjoy a monopoly over the articles in their journals. (If a researcher desperately needs an article published in *Cell*, a subscription to any other journal is useless.) Demand for titles is inherently inelastic, and publishers are free to command whatever prices they choose - schools pretty much have to ante up, until they simply can't afford to pay any more. Annual fees climbing into seven figures saw one UCSF campus cut off from Elsevier's Cell Press journals last fall. Furious researchers demanded a boycott, and Cell Press quickly renegotiated. But the problem remains -- when even massive state schools like UC cringe at subscription tolls, reform is past due.

This publication industry depends entirely upon scientists: our research articles, and our commitment to contribute time and expertise peer-reviewing the work of others are absolutely essential. Amazingly, we provide these crucial commodities to publishers free of charge. Elsevier has never uncovered a single scientific result, but they sure do make a killing selling our own data back to us. Some publishers aren't content to simply look; they've aimed a night-vision zoom-cam directly into the gift horse's mouth.

This fall is an exciting time: the government is finally taking action to ensure public access to taxpayer-funded research. By Dec. 1, the NIH - backed by the U.S. House of Representatives Appropriations Committee - will begin demanding that a full-text copy of every NIH-funded manuscript be deposited in the established PubMed Central repository, available free of charge after a six-month holding period. And that's not all: any article whose publication costs were paid with NIH monies must be made available free of charge, immediately.

This open-archiving plan is a welcome development, addressing the urgent need for some form of taxpayer access to publicly funded basic research. But it does little to ease the burden borne by academic libraries. The requisite six-month embargo, among other considerations, ensures that institutions will still need paid journal subscriptions.

Some publishers are furious over the government directive, bemoaning this interference with free enterprise and their imminent loss of revenue. Elsevier has posted outlandish profits and enjoyed pristine stock ratings for years. Now, the spotlight is on them, the people demand open access, and the party's over. Blame my liberal leanings, but I'm unsympathetic to the cries of a cadre of profiteering monopolists.

If you follow science opinion at all, you're probably familiar with the open-access debate, the upshot being something like this: big corporate publishers are evil but terrific for your career, and upstart open access journals are the squeaky-clean also-rans that won't help your chances of landing a job. The prestige of publishing in the old guard journals is undeniable, and by all accounts, intoxicating.

As students and young researchers, you may not yet enjoy ultimate control over the journals in which you publish. You may prefer to place your personal advancement over public access to your work -- and while the entrenched hierarchy continues to reward this behavior, you'll meet little opposition. But before you fire off that next manuscript to *Cell*, consider this: scientific journals exist to record and disseminate the research results, not to make publishers rich or restrict access to vital information.

Some journals are already working to provide some form of free access to published work -- others steadfastly refuse and fight any government pressure to do so. True open access alternatives do exist, and with the arrival of high-profile journals like *PLoS Biology* they can be quite prestigious indeed. Familiarize yourself with the landscape before choosing sides. As educated scientists, it may be refreshing to consider that where you publish is but a shorthand for the quality of your work.

You do, always, have a choice.

'GOLDEN RECORD' DOES NOT SEND THE RIGHT MESSAGE INTO SPACE

SEPTEMBER 22, 2004

S cientists recently reported that radio transmissions tend to weaken over large distances, leading them to the startling revelation that writing something and mailing it through space is the best way to communicate with aliens. This drew my attention to the two Voyager spacecraft, launched in 1977 -- after all, didn't they carry just such a message?

Indeed, the two Voyager deep-space probes each hold gold-plated copper discs -- called the "Golden Record" -- to be played in a record player (supplied on board) and containing a snapshot of information from Earth. Assuming the aliens can assemble the player and figure out the instructions, they're in for quite a treat: a deep-space personal ad for the entire human race, assembled under the direction of Carl Sagan.

Initially, I found the Golden Record fascinating. How, indeed, do you communicate across untold distances to creatures with no knowledge of your language, writing, symbols, numbering or math?

But while the first couple of plaques are neat -- these deal with basic number systems and offer cryptic heiroglyphic instructions on how to play the records -- the remainder of the album, I am sorry to report, is pretty poor.

I spent quite some time drilling around NASA's Voyager Web site (http://voyager.jpl.nasa.gov), examining the Golden Record. I listened to the "Greetings From Earth" in all 55 languages. I studied the accompanying music selection. The dozens of images depicting life on our planet. The innumerable, confusing line drawings. The list goes on. The result? The collection, overall, is a pretty bland harvest of circa ten thousand years of civilization.

Do you realize that we share collective responsibility, as humans, for sending some poor aliens a mix tape containing about 90 percent classical concertos, rounded out by South American pipe-blowing and "Johnny B Goode"? You can't rage to a single song on there. Any alien is more than justified in showing up on your doorstep clutching this thing and demanding an explanation.

Because we are all equally accountable for this, it behooves us to at least familiarize ourselves with the contents of our messages. For starters, we have the aforementioned music selection, apparently pulled in equal amounts from the discount bin and Carl Sagan's base-ment. Then, we offer greetings saying such things as "Good night ladies and gentlemen, goodbye and see you next time" in Indonesian, and "Friends of space, how are you all? Have you eaten yet? Come visit us if you have time" in the Min dialect Amoy. Strange messages to send to aliens. I guess it doesn't matter, since the aliens likely don't speak Amoy -- but given this, why not say something a little more coy? Playful? Insulting? How about "Aliens are totally not as good as humans!" in Afrikaans or "Bulldog, bulldog bow-wow-wow" in Urdu. The possibilities were truly limitless; NASA really dropped the ball on this one, I think. Also, they apparently commissioned an infant to voice the English greeting, making it very hard to understand.

We arrive now at the collection of images.

These range from random (girl looking in some microscope, cars on a highway) to boring (photos of Jupiter? dude, the aliens can see stuff like that where they are) to really, fully weird. My personal favorite is "Eating and Drinking", a jarring full-color photograph of three smug humans performing hideously exaggerated dinnertime actions. Evidently intended as a simple visual depiction of human food and liquid consumption, this photo instead comes off as a Polaroid-snapped candid from a mental ward. We've only one chance to make a first impression. NASA, please take heed.

The image entitled "Family Ages" is another fine example of good intentions gone hopelessly awry: this image supposedly depicts family members of various ages, silhouetted against a white background, and listing their mass and height. Assuming the goal is noble -- not, say, to give the aliens an idea of the exact cooking time required to broil a human toddler -- the implementation remains atrocious. Armed as I am with a decent grasp of human anatomy, I still concentrated far too long deciphering these shapes. That NASA chose to silhouette squatting, sitting and kneeling people is bad enough -- but what's with all their masses ending in a half-kilogram? I mean, really, the aliens have just learned to read our numbers, and we throw a bunch of fractions at them? Come on, NASA, round it up!

The audio assortment is another gold mine. There are animal noises, and "Sounds of Earth" including such family favorites as "blacksmith dings metal with a hammer," "crying baby" and "jackhammer rattles for 30 seconds." These are noises we try to avoid on Earth. Somehow, mailing them into space doesn't seem like the best idea, especially given the very limited room we have for a message.

Why not send origami instructions, or an Atari? (Aliens should get a big kick out of "Galaxian.")

As it stands, the chances of aliens ever finding this album are pleasantly remote, so the Golden Record is actually little more than human self-reflection on things we consider important, worth preserving and worth communicating. Still, this fails to redeem most of the content. Granted, the math stuff was pretty cool, and some of the animal sounds were alright. But the images are weird and are often incomprehensible, even to humans. The same goes for the music selection and the greetings. Indeed, the majority of the material on the Golden Record pretty much stinks, and it's chilling to think that any one of us might one day be held accountable for mailing this around the universe. Be prepared.

PATENTS ARE OUT OF PLACE ON HUMAN GENOME

DECEMBER 7, 2006

Last fall, the journal Science reported that one-fifth of known human genes have been patented, some as many as 20 times. This surprising result highlights the fact that in America, private entities can now assert ownership over natural phenomena. Even our own genetic constitution is up for grabs.

Genetically, humans vary only slightly. Our genome is a palimpsest reflecting millions of years of speciation and evolution: a sequence of 3 billion nucleotides, 99.9 percent of which is common to all of us. But this shared genomic inheritance is increasingly sequestered by private interests, severely limiting its availability for future biomedical research.

Until recently, living things were insulated from patent claim. In 1948, the Supreme Court ruled that a particular mix of bacteria was "no more than the discovery of some of the handiwork of nature and hence ... not patentable."

This changed in 1980, when the Supreme Court ruling in Diamond v. Chakrabarty allowed the patenting of a genetically engineered microbe useful for cleaning up oil spills. Since then, patents have been obtained for biological material ranging from gene sequences to entire organisms, such as the Harvard OncoMouse.

To understand the problems with this, consider the aim of patents.

The term derives from the Latin patere, meaning "to lay open." Patents are, in effect, limited property rights granted by the government to inventors: In exchange for making public the details of an invention, the patentee is afforded some rights over its use for a number of years. Typically, patent holders exercise this right by excluding others from making, selling or using their invention, or by charging a fee to those who do.

But the human genome is already public: The full sequence and all updates are deposited in freely accessible databases. Here, patented genes present a curious problem. Researchers can look but not touch: Reading the sequence is allowed, but any amplification or assay that crosses patent boundaries is not.

In short, patents - originally conceived to encourage inventors to impart new knowledge to society - are here used for the reverse purpose, to sequester potentially profitable public information and to grant private entities exclusive rights over its use.

Since 2001, patenting a raw nucleotide sequence is no longer allowed. Patents must now include gene function, or demonstrate some novel, non-obvious use for the sequence, like a disease assay. Still, patents are worded as broadly as possible and often have the net effect of obstructing researchers from investigating medically relevant genomic sequence, even for reasons that differ from those stated in the claim.

On Tuesday my colleague Chris Mason, a post-doctoral researcher here at Yale, spoke at a Yale Law School Information Society Project luncheon about the problems of gene patents in a clinical setting.

One example he presented was BRCA1, the famous marker gene patented by Myriad Genetics in 1994. Sequencing this gene in any individual can reveal their susceptibility to breast cancer.

Mason could easily swab your cheek, then amplify and sequence your BRCA1 region in the lab: A few hours and $50 later, he could report your genetic predisposition to breast cancer. But this would constitute patent infringement, as Myriad retains the rights to examine this gene in your body and everyone else's. They sell this same assay for $500.

Sequencing a gene to look for mutations is hardly "non-obvious" to even beginning students of genetics. Yet the BRCA1 patent stands, and many more like it.

So what can be done? At the ISP Luncheon, several ideas were discussed.

The most obvious is simply to challenge Diamond v. Chakrabarty. Much of today's genetic understanding was simply not available when this case was decided. Since 1980, we have moved beyond the "one gene, one protein" hypothesis; we now realize that a single gene can exert broad effects due to pleiotropy, alternate splicing and differential regulation. Genes should not be patented while much of their potential function remains unknown. Direct legal reform, though difficult and sluggish, is the surest way to insulate naturally occurring genomic sequence from patents in future.

Another interesting approach would use the existing patent machinery against itself. If scientists race to patent every possible gene and sequence feature - but attach Creative Commons licenses to each - we could lay claim to a large amount of genetic material and exploit that claim to ward off commercial patents. (The patient advocacy group PXE International pioneered this in 2004, patenting a gene relevant to their illness solely to ensure its continued availability to researchers.)

Patents are designed to cover invention, not scientific discovery. Watson and Crick didn't patent the double helix, Clyde Tombaugh didn't patent Pluto, and Isaac Newton can't bill you whenever an apple falls from a tree. The realities of the natural world are discovered, not created.

Aggressive patenting of human genes is counterproductive. Sequestering public genome information behind corporate curtains impedes taxpayer-funded research. The cost to society is severe.

And yet, the best response may be to file more patents.

Like-minded scientists, unite: Let's patent genetic material for public use, before our entire genome is impounded by private interests.

TECHNOLOGY CAN BREED
DOOMSDAY SCENARIOS

SEPTEMBER 12, 2006

Early next year, the CERN Large Hadron Collider (LHC) will finally commence operation. Buried 100 meters underground near the French-Swiss border, this particle accelerator will send subatomic particles crashing headlong into one another at near light-speed. The resulting high-energy collisions will liberate new particles and illuminate states of matter not seen since the first moments of the universe. Oh, and another thing: This device will spawn a rampant planet-gulping black hole that will devour the Earth and destroy humanity forever.

Doomsayers love particle accelerators. The winning combination of giant machinery, impenetrable quantum jargon and colossal amounts of energy seems to inspire the most vivid predictions of calamity this side of an Al Gore telethon.

In 1995, for instance, University of Hawaii professor Paul Dixon picketed the Fermilab collider in Batavia, Illinois to protest the coming "quantum vacuum collapse" - a doomsday event that would allegedly send a wave of destruction hurtling outwards at the speed of light and obliterate all matter in the universe. In late 1999, just before the Relativistic Heavy Ion Collider (RHIC) opened at Brookhaven National Labs on Long Island, The Sunday Times ran a story entitled "Big Bang Machine Could Destroy Earth." This thoughtful article cautioned that activating RHIC might spawn a thirsty black hole that would tunnel to the Earth's core and blast our planet to bits.

These examples serve to illuminate a fundamental truth of sub-atomic physics: Namely, that the opening of a new particle collider will always be accompanied by dramatic prophecies of world destruction.

When it comes online next spring, the LHC will be the most powerful particle accelerator yet. In a world where higher energy equals more planet-killing terror, this device should invite the most colorful predictions yet.

I scanned the newswires for any warning of impending apocalypse, but the harvest was disappointing. Sure, there's that asteroid set to obliterate the Earth in 200 years, and the global warming shills are doing their very best to alarm the public; but the new particle collider? Not a peep.

How can this be? Here we have perhaps the most egregious threat to the fabric of our universe – this great steel trumpet of doom, this drink in the face of the Natural Order - and the gloom merchants drop the ball?

This simply will not do. The masses need their fear.

Someone needs to cry wolf about this latest, greatest particle accelerator, and it might as well be me. So here goes: The LHC will devastate humanity.

How? Ask any gamer. Thanks to "Doom" and "Quake," the consequences of quantum catastrophe are well known. In fact, what will happen in Geneva next spring has been handily presaged by just about every sci-fi first-person-shooter game ever made. In short: A miscalculation by well-meaning but overconfident scientists will cause a rift in the space-time continuum, opening a dimensional portal and scattering Cyclops, medkits and zombies with rocket launchers throughout every abandoned moonbase in the solar system. A bloody interdimensional war will break out, with heavily-armed and foul-mouthed space marines fighting the last pitched battle for humankind. Before long, this will devolve into chaos - soldiers jumping around like apes on speed, sniping one another furiously and cackling into wireless headsets.

The severity of this outcome really cannot be overstated. Forget black holes; when that collider turns on, anyone without extensive multiplayer training is in dire straits.

Of course, not everyone agrees that the LHC will destroy the world. Some scientists will tell you that there is no danger in particle collision experiments. They will point out that collisions of similar intensity occur in cosmic rays as a matter of course, and that the amount of energy released by the impact of two protons at full speed is roughly equivalent to that of a fly striking a screen door on a still summer night. They will reassure you that any black holes thusly formed are impossibly tiny, and will quickly decay in a burst of Hawking radiation. They will say these things, and you might be tempted to believe them.

You should not. As a scientist myself, I agree that these explanations are enticing. But there is a time to embrace reason, and there is a time to whip the hooded hordes into frenzied, unchecked terror. And this, my friends, is the second kind of time.

So call me a complainer, an irrational cynic, a misanthropic doomster; but come spring, when you're fleeing a dimension-hopping demon with a Gatling gun, just remember - you heard it here first.

REAL SCIENTISTS CAN SPICE UP DESIGN THEORY

FEBRUARY 22, 2007

The horn-rimmed thinkers of this nation are again at odds with the hooded hordes. Evolution is under attack by an energetic fundamentalist right, and these pages are scorched from impassioned sparring over Evolution Sunday. In the face of it all, scientists stubbornly cling to reason: We reject creationism as pseudoscience, and in so doing miss out on countless facile rationalizations and opportunities for intellectual languor. God is not happy.

In the name of all that is good and wholly illogical, scientists must embrace Intelligent Design.

This may seem a tough sell: Intelligent Design is anathema to scientists. Last year, 38 Nobel laureates issued a statement calling the theory "fundamentally unscientific." It has been flatly rejected by the American Association for the Advancement of Science, representing some 120,000 U.S. researchers, and it has been widely panned by virtually every scientific society in existence. The solution, however, is straightforward: If you encounter one of these people, calmly remind them that these views are worth a free drink in hell.

Clearly, I jest. Hell is a religious construction, and Intelligent Design carefully avoids identifying with a specific faith. In reality, naysayers will be relegated to some nondenominational anti-scientific underworld; a land where hypotheses cannot be tested, theories cannot be falsified and data cannot be reproduced. (The usual name for this place is "The Discovery Institute.")

Let's consider the theory. By positing a purposeful creator, Intelligent Design elegantly explains the most complex and exquisite structures in nature. Rest assured, this concept can be made palatable to scientists. We must simply fiddle a bit, and address a few glaring concerns.

The most obvious problem with Intelligent Design is that the configuration of many natural organisms is in fact quite haphazard. Scientists know this. This is because they study nature directly, as opposed to hearing about it in church.

I'd wager most scientists believe the earth was created by a supernatural and mystical being; they just recognize that this being was not, on balance, very smart. Sure, it occasionally displayed intelligence, but mostly it just played games and loafed. Scientists are familiar with this behavior, as they were once college students themselves.

Calling all design "intelligent" is thus too restrictive. To satisfy the empiricists, we shall include four new classes of design.

First, "Bling Design" accounts for those species that mount wanton displays of conspicuous consumption. Peacocks, for instance, sport the phenotypic equivalent of 26-inch spinners with diamond trim. While few would label this an intelligent use of resources, it makes perfect sense if the creator was Thorstein Veblen, or Biggie Smalls.

Next, "Lowest-Bidder Design" produces creatures obviously

streamlined in the name of efficiency. Writhing around on one's belly is not easily described as an intelligent configuration; but as a testament to seventh-day cutbacks, the snake is exquisite in its economy of resources. It bears mention that such design is familiar to contractors and largely unheard of in government.

"Condemned Design" explains those species clearly destined for failure. Dodo birds, woolly mammoths and giant flying reptiles are illustrative examples. Lemmings and Harvard men might safely be included here as well.

The final addition, "Prank Design," covers instances in which organisms are created so they appear to have evolved. An utterly overwhelming majority of natural life falls into this category. The scientific community will cheer this addendum to the design hypothesis. The secret truth is that scientists never really liked Darwin. Evolution was a suboptimal stop-gap, tolerated only until a suitable creationist explanation could be found.

Of course, not every creature can be explained by a single design approach.

Sometimes, combinations are seen. The duckbill platypus, for instance, is a typical example of design by committee.

Having enhanced its ability to explain life on Earth, we now turn to the central logic of Intelligent Design.

A classic complaint is that ID invites tautological question-begging: That is, if life was created by a supernatural being, who designed the designer? This quickly leads to an iterative regression, a logical fallacy which scientists cruelly exploit to discredit the entire theory. Such nit-picking is childish. Clearly the answer is to posit two designers, each of whom created the other. This catch-22 should occupy scientists for many years.

Another problem: Scientists are grossly obsessed with parsimony, the principle of "Occam's Razor." This means they insist on selecting the simplest possible explanation for everything. Doing so leads to less work for them. What they do not realize is that invoking a designer means even less work still, since any conceivable question can now be answered with one reply. As a result, creationist researchers have shorter workdays, longer lunch breaks, and between 30 and 40 weeks of vacation per year. Framed in this way, the theory largely sells itself.

Church-science strife is so Renaissance, and by Renaissance I mean barbaric and passe. Scientists, let's lose the gung-ho work ethic and quench our piddling curiosity about the natural world. It's time to embrace a more sophisticated view: one where complicated systems are instinctively deemed "irreducibly complex" and avoided in favor of simpler problems, or a round of mini-putt.

In seriousness, I do think scientists should seize Intelligent Design and revise it heavily. That way, even if all life isn't the work of intelligent beings — well, at least the theory will be.

ACADEMICS

DIPLOMA MILLS DESERVE THEIR OWN RANKINGS

APRIL 5, 2007

In early April, US News and World Report released the 2008 ranking of American Graduate Schools. Diploma mills — unaccredited colleges that award degrees with little or no study — were not included.

More and more Americans are buying credentials online, but faced with a staggering array of phony schools, how is the aspiring charlatan to choose?

Ranking fake schools presents an interesting challenge. Traditional metrics break down rather quickly when applied to an online facade with no faculty, no courses and no fixed address. So I explored a few dozen sites, devised some categories and ranked schools in each. Here, I present the six winners of my very own Best Diploma Mills survey.

Most Brazen: InstantDegrees.com. Many diploma mills strive to look semi-professional. Not this one. The main page is a rabbit-hole to a Wonderland of amusing content, like a scathing denunciation of academics who "frittered away years in classrooms" just to "use the same title or post-nominal letters that you can legally acquire in a matter of days for the price of a meal in a decent restaurant." Damn. Now you tell me!

The "order now" page is free of pretense. No inventing life histories or submitting dissertations here; simply choose the degree title (bachelor's, master's or doctorate), subject area and your desired graduation date. InstantDegrees.com is cheap — $130 for a B.A. and $180 for a Ph.D. — but because of "legal loopholes" you cannot know which school will actually award your degree until you pay for it. Sounds mysterious, until you learn that all degrees bought here ultimately come from "Buxton University" and are mailed from Portugal.

Best Public Image Snafu: Trinity Southern University. This Texas-based two-man show made headlines in 2004 when it awarded an executive MBA to a cat. The cat's owner, a deputy attorney general in Pennsylvania, promptly sued the school for fraud. It no longer exists.

Best Hometown Player: Suffield University. Several directories of known diploma mills list this school "operating illegally in Connecticut." Suffield's site offers a list of majors including Fire Science, though I suspect you can get fired with any of their degrees.

Best Actual Campus: Hamilton University. A deserted Motel 6 in Evanston, Wyoming, served as the campus for this diploma mill, while an empty church across the parking lot qualified it for tax-exempt status. In 2004, 60 Minutes visited and requested a campus tour. The lone employee "locked the door and called police." Shortly thereafter Hamilton was ruled illegal in Wyoming and is now operating as Richardson University in the Bahamas. Trivia: Hamilton is best known for awarding three degrees (B.A., M.A. and Ph.D.) to Homeland Security official Laura Callahan.

Most Famous Alumni: Columbia Pacific University. Dr. John Gray, best-selling author of "Men are from Mars, Women are from Venus" has a Ph.D. from this now-defunct California-based school. Blogger Kieran Healy summed it up nicely: "Men from Mars, Women from Venus, PhDs from Uranus."

Most Immersive Fiction: Belford, Rochville and Ashwood universities (tie). With slick (and strangely similar) Web sites, these three schools each claim accreditation by official-sounding agencies with separate Web sites. However, the Texas Higher Education Coordinating Board noted last year that these schools and their respective accrediting groups are in fact all run by the same people. They take great pains to appear legitimate: Belford University boasts deliciously phony alumni such as "Luke Jonathan, a Belford Doctorate" recently promoted to director of the nonexistent "Archbeal Solutions, Inc." Belford at one point maintained a P.O. Box in Humble, Texas, but degrees from all three schools ship from the United Arab Emirates.

Just how hard is it to earn an "accredited Ph.D." online? Using a pseudonym, I applied for a doctorate from Belford University. For subject area, I typed "prestige." My justification for this credential was brief, stating mainly that "I have held a number of extremely prestigious posts," "I am known as Mr. Prestige a lot of the time" and "now I need to be Dr. Prestige." I also claimed "a brief music career which I would describe as prestigious."

Based on this "life experience," I was informed by e-mail 12 hours later that the "10-member evaluation committee" had approved my petition. My doctorate will cost $549. A 3.0 GPA is free, though for $25 more I can buy Latin honors; an extra $75 lets me backdate the degree. The package includes an official-looking diploma, concocted transcripts and even a telephone verification service so employers can confirm that I am, in fact, Dr. Prestige.

Match that, Yale!

If this seems harmless, consider: More than 2,000 diploma mills are currently operating, generating over $500 million in annual revenue. A 2004 report by the Government Accountability Office revealed nearly 500 senior federal employees listing diploma mill degrees among their qualifications, many of whom have top-secret security clearance and remain in those jobs today. (In some cases, federal funds were used to pay diploma mill "tuition.") The GOA concluded that the true number of civil servants with bogus degrees is likely far higher. No crackdown has yet materialized.

This tacit endorsement of purchased credentials suggests diploma mills are here to stay, and most of us will encounter their handiwork in years to come. To determine whether a degree or accrediting agency is recognized, the (quite real) Council for Higher Education Accreditation maintains a searchable database.

But for now, the fun is just starting. So here's to phony degrees, and a new breed of college rankings.

TRUMP-ING A YALE EDUCATION? NOT QUITE

SEPTEMBER 15, 2005

F orget Harvard: We're under attack from a new foe. On June 28, Roger Schank wrote that many Yale courses "clearly have no relevance" to our future lives. The former Yale computer science professor lamented the fact that here, students earn credits in such trivialities as ASTR420a, "Computational Methods for Astrophysics" and WGSS 295a, "Women and Gender in a Transnational Context," without a single semester-hour spent on the art of the deal or nothing-down real-estate investment. He was evidently so frustrated with the shortage of capitalist dogma in our core curriculum that he joined the faculty of Trump University (as "Chief Learning Officer") and from this glass house now lobs his stones.

I sat on my hands and held my breath, but Yale has yet to respond; so, stung by the dig -- and drunk on power as a News columnist -- I find myself saddled with the solemn duty to fire a salvo at the academic comb-over that is Trump U.

Trump University -- motto: "We Teach Success" -- is devoted to the dogged pursuit of material self-interest. It awards no diplomas, and seems mostly to offer seminars and audio programs on personal improvement and wealth creation. Eager to learn more (and who wouldn't be?), I visited www.trumpuniversity.com. I registered immediately for e-mail updates -- using the ultra-clever nom de plume "D. Trump" and resisting, for the time being, the urge to order a YOU'RE FIRED mug -- and have since received nearly a dozen missives promising immediate wealth and insider secrets from the king of capitalism himself.

Donald Trump has amassed a considerable fortune in his lifetime. While not alone in this, he is unrivaled in his insatiable need to parade his wealth. He routinely emblazons his name on everything from shimmering buildings to commercial jets, a show of pretension that would make Gordon Gekko cringe. Still, these prior offenses pale in comparison with his Web site, www.trump.com. For those with a moment to spare between irrelevant Yale classes, I heartily recommend a tour. Watch enthralled as an ostentatious Flash intro, complete with orchestral sound track, segues to Trump's satisfied smirk. Marvel at "Donald Trump: The Fragrance," and don't miss the advertisement for "Trump Ice" bottled water.

Trump's megalomania leaves no stone unturned; he has even commissioned a scandalously ornate coat of arms for himself, which truly must be seen to be appreciated. This crest and his own face are plastered on every available space around the Web site, and a digitized version of his signature is liberally applied throughout. (Precisely what he is signing, or what assurances we are to take from this, is unclear.) The resulting experience is part Vegas, part Comedy Central. The more Trump strives for authenticity, the more he belies his spurious mystique. In one sense though, our awe is genuine: As a study in bombast, this site is without peer. We are rightly humbled by his utter meisterstück of self-aggrandizing rodomontade.

In short, Trump's self-promotion is now a business in itself. I do wonder what secrets The Donald professes in his lectures, since so much of his current success stems from trading on his own name -- obviously not a tactic the rest of us are poised to mimic.

Trump U could be an amusing diversion, if not for Schank's destructive message: that a true college education is functionally ir-relevant. This idea appears frequently in get-rich-quick material, of necessity. Simply put, every wealth-building guru must ultimately seduce a poor, uneducated audience. Many do so by adopting the ethos of "Rich Dad, Poor Dad" author Robert Kiyosaki; namely, empowering the unschooled by attacking, criticizing and ultimately dismissing traditional education. Such snake oil is no doubt tantaliz-ing for those who did poorly in school and yearn to strike it rich, but it's misleading. Yes, basic financial concepts are omitted from high school curricula to ill effect, as the waxing debt crisis now illustrates; but to claim this cancels the value of a traditional college education is a red herring. Statistically, the most reliable predictor of high income remains a college degree, and I don't expect Trump U to impact this trend anytime soon. Employers might not "expect anyone to have learned anything relevant at Yale," but as Schank complains, they still seem quite eager to hire us.

Ultimately, Schank's critique is hollow. At a university, knowl-edge is pursued without the omnipresent tether to material gain; it's therefore disingenuous to label as trivial any subject for which no im-mediate profit motive asserts itself. Further, a Yale education is more than the sum of its courses: The academic material taught here could surely be ingested by other means, but our experience in doing so would be greatly diminished. It's difficult to imagine our education without the history, traditions, clubs and architecture that surround us; and harder still to fathom one stripped of the most important factor of all: the students, scholars and assorted lunatics who work and study alongside us. More than anything else, this cacophony of voices, histories and interests defines our time at Yale. And this is one area in which Trump U will simply never compare.

And if that's not enough, well, Yale has bottled water, too.

APTITUDE GAUGES ARE OFTEN SKEWED

SEPTEMBER 22, 2006

Many years ago, I learned the so-called "Golden Rule" of biochemistry: You get what you assay for. In other words, the result you attain from an experiment depends upon what you measure. This is a basic lesson and a good one, one that college admissions staff would do well to remember.

Harvard's retreat from Early Decision this fall has called public attention to a larger problem in college admissions: With the twin goals of enrolling better students and climbing in the rankings, colleges have quietly morphed into high-throughput sorting machines, judging applicants very efficiently on questionable criteria.

Earning a spot at a top school has become quite the undertaking indeed. We've all met students who stacked their extracurricular dance cards from an early age, and others whose devotion to high school volunteerism was perhaps not entirely selfless. We know those who studied fanatically for standardized tests, and we've all heard of high-priced admissions experts grooming applicants for an Ivy nod. In a world where everything can be gamed, what pure metrics remain?

Admissions committees employ a few key measures to assess academic ability, intellectual promise, community dedication and whatever else. But the playing field is tilted, favoring those with the time and money to boost their scores, hire essay advisors and otherwise whack every mole. An applicant who cannot afford such luxuries is effectively consigned to a lower percentile rank by the many thousands who can.

I had a recent brush with this phenomenon last December, when I decided to apply to law school. Clueless, bigheaded or both, I took the LSAT pretty much cold. My thinking was that because the exam is designed to test not rote knowledge but some vague idea of general aptitude, little would be gained by studying. As the hordes now gearing up for the September sitting will no doubt attest, this was a trifle optimistic.

Since taking the exam, I've spoken with a good number of people at the other end of the spectrum: those who spent many months drilling questions, shelled out a small fortune for LSAT courses, rehearsed every possible type of logic game and predictably did exceptionally well - far better than their initial timed diagnostic. It's not a miracle cure, but dedicated preparation undoubtedly boosts test scores. Many prep courses guarantee it.

If standardized tests can be gamed - even a little - by those with time and money to devote to extensive preparation, they're not the great equalizer we think they are.

Sifting through such inequalities is the job of admissions committees, and they're surely very good at it. The whole problem might end right there, if the committee's freedom to assemble a class were not curbed by outside pressure.

Perhaps more than any other single factor, reliance on the U.S. News and World Report college rankings has polluted the admissions process. By evaluating every college with the same superficial criteria, trumpeting the result as the one true barometer of academic quality and convincing society to buy into it all, this publication has irrevocably damaged the academic landscape in the United States.

Rankings are mostly harmless until colleges heed them. Once schools begin altering their admissions behavior to improve their standing, a feedback loop is formed. The driving force in admissions is no longer just assembling the best possible class; it is now to assemble the best class that will also look the best on paper.

The problem with this is that by amassing aggregate values, rankings cannot help but de-contextualize any information they present. This encourages schools themselves to divorce standardized test scores from the remainder of an applicant's package and apply cutoffs and absolute limits - an approach that doesn't make sense given the basic intent of the tests.

Test scores matter, in an absolute sense, because rankings pressure schools to court and enroll the highest-scoring students. A pricey game can be played to boost test scores. Some, constrained by job, family or finance, can't afford to play.

This is the very same inequality that eventually condemned early decision, a process that compels applicants to commit to a school before seeing its financial aid offer. Harvard's move will be widely copied, and this is a good thing: Doing so removes one barrier from a system that has become increasingly geared toward high-income applicants.

As good meritocratic citizens, we rightly reject the notion that a privileged upbringing should sway an admissions panel. But remember the Golden Rule: If we define aptitude as the ability to cram all summer and game an exam on daddy's nickel, then sorting applicants by standardized test score will indeed select for very apt people. Anyone with a summer job or bills to pay is just out of luck. You get what you assay for.

The solution here is simple. Schools must admit classes as they choose, without mind to how each score will affect some artificial collegiate ranking. Doing so keeps scores in proper context and human judgment in charge.

College classes shouldn't reflect social class. In college admissions, let's not exalt criteria that can be gamed by kids at the top.

US News rankings are as inert as the Constitution

November 7, 2007

It's application season — time for turkey, eggnog and a look at the academic rankings.

The US News and World Report rankings are low-hanging fruit for columnists. Countless writers have criticized the study for methodological skulduggery, over-reliance on manipulable criteria, favoring small schools and whatever else. Yet, I've seen students agonize over their school's placement in the coming year, dreading further drops or praying for a rally. Just this week, I came to a realization.

We can all stop scrutinizing. No matter what happens at the actual schools, it's very unlikely that the substantive rankings will ever meaningfully change.

Why? Because the US News rankings are very much like the Constitution and the Uniform Commercial Code. And anyone who saw that coming just earned my respect and sympathy in roughly equal measure.

What common thread binds the fundamental law of the United States, a uniform act that standardizes the law of commercial transactions and an arbitrary, over-used sorting matrix for largely incomparable academic institutions?

Each filled a yawning void in its time. Before each, the world was a vague and messy place. And what's striking about all three documents is their resultant stability.

First, the Constitution. For a newly independent land with no central government, confederation meant stability, binding the states for their common defense and welfare. There was an obvious push to get something on the books and ratified rather quickly; virtually any document that accomplished the main objectives was decidedly better than nothing. The Articles of Confederation was a good first stab, but its weaknesses were many. In 1788 the Articles were supplanted by the more thorough U.S. Constitution — a document legendary in its stability. Of the roughly 10,000 amendments proposed since 1789, only 27 have been ratified, 10 of those in the first two years. A good chunk of constitutional jurisprudence these days involves convoluted intellectual acrobatics construing aged passages to allow or disallow some decidedly modern action.

The Constitution quickly became entrenched, relied upon, known. Interests have staked out positions on either side of its words. To fundamentally revise or even freshly interpret the text today would meet intense resistance: just imagine the Supreme Court actually ruling on whether the Second Amendment really does confer the right of individual citizens to keep and bear arms: an uphill battle in either direction.

I'll spare readers the history of the UCC, but suffice to say that a similar process occurred. Before its adoption in the 1950s the law governing simple commercial transactions was a mess, often highly inconsistent between states. There was a very real benefit to a common and uniform standard, regardless of what that standard might be; So long as it was largely fair and achieved the goal of synthesizing the confusing pile of common law, it would be an improvement. Details could surely be ironed out later.

Except they couldn't.

Since its adoption, attempts to revise the code have largely been frustrated. Parties rarely agree on revisions to the various rules; changes that benefit consumers are opposed by corporate interests, and vice versa. Although Article 2 revisions were finally proposed in 2003, only two states have moved to adopt them. Since the primary benefit of any uniform law is its uniformity, the system decays when states adopt revisions piecemeal. Once the first draft was out there, similarly uniform updates were just wishful thinking.

And that is precisely why school rankings won't change much. By popularizing their hierarchy of colleges, law schools and whatever, US News captured people's uncertain notions of academic reputation (once confined to a few "top" schools and a general sense of how local institutions might compare), added some rudimentary statistics and squeezed from it all an ordinate list. This list filled a void: It allowed people to affirm vague conceptions of "better than" and "worse than" and anchor them to a master document. The published ranking quickly supplanted the public opinion that hatched it and became the touchstone of academic quality. Today, the rankings are too widely used to change with the times.

Any substantial disruption of the rankings as we know them would be rejected as roundly as a major rewrite of the UCC. If the top schools were suddenly upset by a surge of also-rans, many would simply disown the US News list as rogue, and turn to another source that better reflected what we have come to accept.

The obvious message is to take the rankings with caution — at this point, they likely reflect stubborn inertia at least as much as meaningful quality.

But there is also a certain Frankenstein angle to all this — once unleashed, common standards take on a life of their own. So be careful, all ye Yalies who sully forth into positions of boundless power this year and beyond: when you tame the world with some hot new paradigm, think well on the first draft — your monster can be a nightmare to revise.

POLITICS

TOLERANCE, SENSITIVITY AND RESPECT? OH MY!

JANUARY 31, 2005

Attention, citizens. Your nation is on Gay Alert.

It's true: On Jan. 20, MSNBC wire service reported that two Christian groups had issued a "gay alert warning" over an upcoming television special featuring SpongeBob SquarePants. I followed the ensuing ruckus with understandable rapture, for not only was I unfamiliar with "SpongeBob SquarePants" -- something that sounds more like an embarrassing infection than a children's cartoon -- but I was most definitely a stranger to the Gay Alert.

Query the issue online and you'll uncover a heated discussion, centered around a short video which allegedly features SpongeBob, Barney and myriad other Freudian nightmares singing "We are Family"; this video was produced by the conveniently-named We Are Family Foundation and is destined for -- gasp! -- schoolchildren. I hope this doesn't sound in any way benign, because good golly, it's not.

To my dismay, initial reports were misleading: The Christians never accused SpongeBob himself of being queer. No, he's just a jolly, upbeat sponge who lives in a pineapple under the sea, and the jury's still out on him. But what, then, was SpongeBob's crime? Caught in a compromising tangle with Winnie the Pooh? Snapped slapping rainbow decals on senators' limos? No, my gentle flock -- SpongeBob is guilty of promoting tolerance of homosexuality.

Christian groups are outraged, and led by the cringe-worthy duo of the "American Family Association" and "Focus on the Family," they have issued boycotts and screamed polemical Mayday. Beware the homo sponge! Ahem, sorry -- beware the words of compassion brought by the pineapple-dwelling heathen! Quick, raise the Gay Alert level to Rainbow!

Permit me a brief reality check in this foaming maelstrom of Big-Gulp idiocy: Tolerance is defined as the capacity to recognize and respect the beliefs or practices of others. I'll repeat this, because it's important: "Recognize and respect." Not adopt, condone or even endorse. Startlingly, this distinction has not escaped the Christian right, who lambasted the authors of the video for their vow of tolerance: "I pledge to have respect for people whose abilities, beliefs, culture, race, sexual identity or other characteristics are different from my own." A threatening mantra if ever I heard one. Them's fightin' words.

Evidently, the nation must accept that not only are so-called Moral Moms deathly afraid of their children turning out queer, but they reject the notion that their kids can even tolerate gays. And good for them! Since when was tolerance the teaching of the Lord, anyway?

Christian groups, flying the twin banners of morality and family values, have attacked the belief that homosexuals deserve respect. They have whipped God-fearing parents into a homophobic frenzy, leveling pre-emptive embargoes and browbeating school boards to reject the cartoon. AFA chairman Don Wildmon has even condemned an online petition that encouraged signers to combat "ignorance, insensitivity and bigotry." By golly, I'm glad someone put a stop to that!

Up with ignorance, insensitivity and bigotry, praise the Lord!

This all reminds me of the scandal several years back, wherein Teletubby Tinky-Winky was "outed" by the Christian right, presumably for carrying a purse and being popular with homosexuals. The utter hilarity of the recent SpongeBob Gay Alert, paired with the unsmiling righteousness with which it was issued, begs the question -- where does the next homosexual threat lurk? The terrific thing about this is, of course, that the simplest way to send rednecks fleeing for cover is to claim their interests are appealing to gays. Imagine the pure havoc that would grip the South following a Fox News update that NASCAR has become the sport of choice for urban gays, or that bourbon is preferred 2-to-1 by homosexuals. Pandemonium!

Flatly stated, the angst of the religious right is absurd: Homosexuality is not the norm for the human race, and by definition, can never be. It is not rampant or dangerous, and tolerance of homosexuals is at worst wholly benign. In all seriousness, what do they fear will happen if SpongeBob hits the schools with his wild words? Worst case, the next generation of Americans isn't quite so prone to bigotry.

And yet, the alert stands. We live in preposterous times: times where the continued persecution of gays, the poor and immigrants is a "moral" issue, but an unjust war somehow is not; where Creationist theme parks blithely display humans walking amidst dinosaurs; where a smug president spends millions on tasteless self-indulgence while his troops perish far away for want of Humvee armor.

The moderate center is losing this battle of attrition. It's trench warfare. Here, we see an attack not on gays, but on widespread acceptance of gays. This is patent rubbish, and must be stopped.

And to you, Don Wildmon, listen. I'm hardly an advocate of cartoon sponges with single-digit IQs blathering nonsense to the nation's youth; and I agree, if anything sounds like a Gay Alert waiting to happen, it's this video. But fear SquarePants - not the real, breathing people he begs us all to tolerate.

REPUBLICANS ARE TO BLAME FOR FOLEY'S FOLLY

OCTOBER 5, 2006

Florida Republican Congressman Mark Foley last week moonwalked away from his special Neverland of alleged man-boy seduction, leaving us to ponder a thorny question: Precisely how busy must an elected representative be before masturbation takes a back seat to politics?

Thanks to transcripts and ABC News' intrepid reporting, we need no longer puzzle over this. Quoth Foley to the school-age congressional page boy: I am "never too busy" to "spank it." Ah, your tax dollars at work.

What a mess. The so-called "family values" party caught with its pants down - in the office, no less. (Karma-hungry Clintonites, suppress your cheers.) A bona fide sexual predator co-chairing the House Committee on Missing and Exploited Children; a full record of his lewd online chatter splashing about the public domain - its release cruelly timed to inflict maximum election-season damage on the GOP.

So it should. The Foley transcripts are like emetic in print. Featuring novel positions for auto-stimulation, an unwelcome return of the term "horndog" and an unexplained cast fetish, the grossly familiar and playful gushing with minors is jarring. Stripped of these talking points, what remains is a sad story of a closeted gay man confined by a strict ideological harness to play out stifled fantasies on the Web.

The public release of the bawdy chats prompted Foley's swift resignation and a torrent of curious mea culpa. First, Foley stole a page (forgive me) from Mel Gibson's book. Nabbed in a July drunk-stop, everyone's favorite lethal weapon disavowed his evident anti-Semitism, blaming it all on the bottle. Foley too has committed himself to rehab, a move which, in addition to presumably weaning him from drink and young boys, has the convenient side effect of sheltering him from the media for a 30 day cooldown.

The rehab visit is a stunt. I know more than one habitual abuser of alcohol, and never to my knowledge has a happy hour binge caused any of them to suddenly drool over the lacrosse team, or send spicy text-messages to blazer-clad high-schoolers.

Foley's salacious urges have nothing to do with alcohol abuse, and everything to do with the oppressive, closet-slamming culture of the American right. That the man only confessed his homosexuality as the final footnote to a major Washington scandal is telling: To be gay and Republican is an obvious no-no. It's troubling to think that this otherwise successful fellow evidently submerged his innate sexual leaning for decades just to please a pitiless clan of queer-fearing old-boys.

As any Freud fan will attest, to frustrate sexual desire is a stopgap; suppressed feelings will surface in devious ways. I'd wager that young Foley always had the hots for the lacrosse team. This desire lingered and eventually bubbled forth into the vast lawless void of the online landscape, where until last week, he indulged with impunity and relative innocence that which he had so long sought.

That Foley simultaneously headed the Caucus on Catching People like Himself will be seized upon as grand and vile hypocrisy. In reality, I doubt it was anything more than sincere atonement for his "sinful" appetites - working publicly to combat those urges he was taught to despise in himself.

Ah, amateur psychoanalytic assessment by an unqualified News columnist. You know what they say: That and $4.50 will get you a cafe latte. By all accounts, Foley had no physical sexual contact with the boys; his misbehavior was restricted to lascivious chat. I can't imagine he would have made such bold advances in person or via phone. Perhaps the real story is the seductive isolation of Internet chat: Spontaneity, false intimacy and enduring, easily-shared transcripts make Instant Messaging a honey-pot for scandal. The lesson: Don't type anything online you wouldn't send to your mother. On letterhead.

With the newly-minted predator safely sequestered in rehab, his attorney called a press conference and announced "Mark Foley wants you to know, he is a gay man." I like to think Foley offered this late confession not to excuse his behavior - after all, the idea gay men inevitably favor illicit online trysts with underage politicos is neither pleasant nor tenable - but to ensure every shred of his dirty laundry was aired en masse. No sense settling in at the clinic only to realize he's forgotten to shut off the stove, forward calls or out himself on national television.

GOP heavies will never concede their draconian attachment to sexual homogeneity (a family value, you know) perhaps played a part in turning Foley rogue. Their evangelical bedrock will not permit it: These are the folk who shun Spongebob for promoting tolerance of gays and endorse "conversion" of homosexuals.

No, the disgraced congressman will be excommunicated and strung from the highest tree - quickly recast as a sick sexual predator, imposter, treacherous deviant. His lapse will be twisted to further vilify homosexuality and to shore up the same boorish dogma that warped him to begin with.

Let the carnage begin. It is with special wrath that the falsely righteous turn upon their own.

DENMARK SHOULD STAND BY FIREBRAND CARTOONISTS

FEBRUARY 2, 2006

The Muslim world is up in arms over cartoons. A bizarre incident involving caricatures of Mohammed in a Danish daily paper has angered Islamic leaders, escalated to international proportions and threatens to spark legitimate conflict. Amid threats of violence, Denmark must now stand in defense of its most puerile citizens.

The trouble began in September when the Danish newspaper Jyllands-Posten published a dozen cartoons depicting Mohammed, including one in which the prophet's turban is shaped like a bomb. These cartoons were solicited from various artists as an exercise in self-censorship, apparently to see how far cartoonists would go in styling the Islamic holy figure.

Since any depiction of Mohammed is considered blasphemous, there is little question that the paper was tempting trouble by publishing the drawings. The editors obviously sought to raise a few eyebrows, or perhaps even tousle some Middle Eastern plumage. Instead, they provoked a major diplomatic snafu.

Last Friday, a Saudi Arabian prayer leader condemned the images in a widely-broadcast sermon, igniting uproar. Within days, a tempest was brewing in a Danish demi-tasse. Saudi Arabia withdrew its ambassador from Denmark; Lybia closed its embassy entirely. Protestors in Gaza have begun torching images of Danish Prime Minister Anders Fogh Rasmussen. A telephoned bomb threat forced evacuation of the Jyllands-Posten offices on Tuesday, shortly after a militant Islamic Web site pledged violent reprisals. Danish citizens have been urged to avoid Arab nations, several of which are now arranging to boycott Danish goods.

Regardless of its modest origin, this incident has spun out of control: what began as a publishing gaffe has become a serious international imbroglio.

What can be done to resolve the mess? The cartoons can hardly be un-published. No remedy exists for any damage they may have caused; the only real option is to beg the pardon of Muslims worldwide and hope the issue dies down. On Tuesday the Jyllands-Posten issued a lengthy front-page apology in Danish, English and Arabic, but this gesture had the appearance of being too little, too late. It failed to calm the rising storm, since the target of reproach has since shifted -- Arab nations and Muslim groups are demanding a full apology from the Danish government.

Prime Minister Rasmussen has thus far stood firm, insisting that his government cannot apologize on behalf of an independent newspaper that acted within the limits of Danish law. Good for him; he would be wrong to concede.

However ill-advised these cartoons may have been, and however unfortunate their impact on the Muslim community, they were nonetheless the work of a free press. Since the images were not deemed hateful by the courts, to backpedal as a nation from their appearance in the news is to contradict the fundamental notion of free expression.

In principle, defending free speech is easy. But in practice, doing so almost always involves wading into a bitter quarrel where repugnant views have been expressed, and opposing those who would silence them. And while we are all no doubt familiar with Voltaire's distinction between embracing an opinion and defending the right to put it forth, it's surprising how easily, when tempers flare, these blur. Try it out: Defend free speech in any instance where it is actually in peril, and you will surely be accused of siding with the provocateur.

Nonetheless, if we are serious about freedom of expression, we accept this risk; we must be willing to enter the fray to defend the expression of views we do not endorse. As Noam Chomsky says, to support free speech in any meaningful sense means doing so precisely for views you despise.

Denmark's record of religious freedom and tolerance speaks for itself, and any who seek to paint the government as systemically hostile to Islam are likely to come up empty-handed. The sudden vilification of Denmark is particularly absurd considering the fact that demonstrated anti-Muslim hostility in the US media has prompted no boycott of FOX or McDonald's, and Israeli goods continue to line shelves across the Mideast despite that nation's penchant for bloody clashes with Arab populations. The coordinated Muslim response to a Danish cartoon is impressive, but oddly misdirected.

Nevertheless, the chaos is real. In refusing to issue a national apology, Prime Minister Rasmussen will be accused of brinksmanship, stubbornness and, in all likelihood, endorsing religious discrimination. He must remain resolute -- for while the appearance of these images was regrettable, they do not empower him to deem freedom of expression a flexible concept. Braving shampoo boycotts, bomb threats and deserted embassies, the Danes must now stand fast.

But when this fracas settles, that Danish newspaper really does deserve a slap. Free speech or not, we accept that certain topics -- the Holocaust, for instance -- are sure to irritate and are best left alone. Jyllands-Posten editors have flouted taboo, set off an international spat, and roused us, reluctant, to their defense.

It gives us no pleasure to martyr such boors on the altar of free speech, but as is so often the case, it must be done.

You can't help but sigh.

ELECTION-WISE, I'M A STRANGER IN A STRANGE LAND

NOVEMBER 3, 2004

As a Canadian living in America, electoral frustration and political impotence are de rigeur for me. Like you natives, we foreign nationals are swamped by television advertisements, furious campaigning and a tempest of debate; yet only we are denied the sole cathartic moment of the entire process, that empowering lever-pulling theophany at the vote-casting machine. However, an increasing number of my American friends now display precisely the same irritation, political ex-pats in their own land. This isn't so hard to understand: For the past few months, virtually everyone I know was either scrambling to deify one of two startlingly similar candidates, or steadily building immunity to a mounting barrage of persuasion.

You Americans do confuse me. Your fanatical devotion to a two-party system is alien to me, and the bounding of debate in this country is spectacular. The one candidate who routinely embraces nontraditional views was drummed off the stage, and the mere mention of

Nader still drives many Democrats to frenzy. Perhaps I haven't lived here long enough, and my indoctrination is not yet complete; nevertheless, slamming a candidate for daring to run, daring to "steal" votes from the established left, seems to me a complete mockery of democracy. Sure, in Canada our ballots occasionally read like comic strips: Each riding sports its own idiosyncratic independent and playfully named candidates, and established outliers -- like the Marijuana Party and the Natural Law Party (which endorses "Yogic flying" as a panacea for world troubles) -- always command a few hopeful votes. Is a vote cast for the Marijuana Party entirely trivial? Perhaps. But is any vote for a fresh new candidate automatically a squandered ballot? At the very least, this certainly isn't up to the sitting government to decide: After all, self-perpetuating governments resilient to removal are the antithesis of democracy.

What strikes me about voter apathy here is the popular notion among undecided voters that no matter who wins, nothing will really change. Pause to consider this, and you will find it remarkably, fundamentally true. Neither Bush nor Kerry even suggests it was incorrect to invade Iraq. Neither will so much as fondle the grossly obese Pentagon budget, much less combat the actual obesity epidemic in America. Neither will provide significant respite to the working poor; neither has suggested a serious welfare system, and neither would dare to offer the much-demonized "socialized health care" Canadians enjoy (and I do mean enjoy). Neither will deal with Cuba, and neither will repeal the first-strike policy governing the thousands of nuclear warheads currently standing ready on 15-minute alert. Neither will submit to world government in any meaningful way, and, too constrained by the need to satisfy the interests of major corporations, neither candidate can afford to espouse real environmental reform. I will not suggest that all of these things must necessarily change, but if you happen to care deeply about any one of these issues, you're out of luck: They're simply not on the table. Your choices are abortion, taxes and health-care premiums. End of debate.

The fundamental agreement between Democrats and Republicans on so many key issues begs a question, and I'm going to ask it: What happens if we consider both parties as the dual faces of a single social elite? Well, we'd expect airwaves blanketed with propaganda, careful selection of certain topics for debate, collusion and taboo avoidance of other issues, and a strong resistance to any outside political challengers. In times of serious political decision-making, such as the weeks following 9/11 or the beginning of war in Iraq, we'd expect these two parties to rally together, uniting in common interest at the very time when stakes are high and debate should be most vigorous. Arguably, supporting either party does carry with it silent support of a great number of highly questionable socioeconomic assumptions. It all gets very Orwellian, very fast: The end result is a maelstrom of mudslinging and circular reasoning that leaves the average citizen overwhelmed, exhausted, isolated and understandably unenthusiastic about endorsing any candidate. Voter turnout consistently hovers around 50 percent.

Meanwhile, disproportionately enthusiastic (and puzzlingly named) "get out the vote" campaigns combat apathy by flogging the benighted masses to the polls. I'm all in favor of easy access, but the tactics employed in pursuit of this year's projected record turnout are truly startling: The New York Times reported Tuesday that gangs of canvassers employing "knock-and-drag" coercion scoured neighborhoods across the country in rented vans, hustling unwitting citizens to polling stations. Being really controversial for a moment, let's allow that perhaps not every American shares the views of either presidential contender, and let's further allow that perhaps these citizens are not lazy but are actually unwilling to endorse one or the other as their elected leader. Given this possibility, how will historians view the knock-and-drag gangs, the free tacos, extra credit in courses and other perks that accompany the rote endorsement of the two-party system? (I'm not making those up, by the way.) Volunteers, answer me this -- is it really your civic duty to coerce others into a lose-lose decision by endorsing a leader they would not otherwise support?

For a nation that prides itself as a pillar of democracy and freedom, debate seems sharply constrained here, and your real choices as citizens are very limited. Of course, the standard rebuttal to all this is to dismiss political hegemony as a response to public will, claiming that corporations and parties merely give the citizens what they want. This is a convenient fiction and a pleasing one, and will persist so long as no real options exist to assay it. After all, it's impossible to know how this election might have turned out, divorced from the months of partisan spin and incessant harping on carefully selected topics.

So who cares what a Canadian thinks about your elections, anyway? Probably no one, but I ask what difference your own views made yesterday if they didn't fit nicely into one of the two glossy political receptacles available to you.

Likely, you found yourself either casting a guilty vote for a doomed candidate, or like so many others, just disenfranchised, unsatisfied and reluctant to vote at all, hounded to the polls by fanatical and predatory canvassers.

So go ahead, dismiss these views as the crazed ramblings of a foreign national. Like you, I'm just glad I don't have to see "I'm George W. Bush, and I approved this message" ever again.

YOUR TRUTH OR MINE?
ANSWER: RELATIVISM

SEPTEMBER 29, 2005

E arlier this week, Peter Johnston condemned relativism and suggested that America must "regain the conviction of the exclusivity of truth" ("Shift to relativism spells end for truth," 9/27). It's refreshing to see some first-principles philosophical debate in these pages, a good old contentious free-for-all. However, in a social context, a stalwart belief in absolute truth is restrictive, exclusive and potentially damaging -- far more threatening than any relativist stance.

As a disclaimer, I should mention that I approach this topic as a layman and will sidestep the obvious logical potholes (such as the impossibility of refuting absolute truth without invoking absolute truth in your argument) to take issue primarily with Johnston's contention that we need more absolutes in society and government. While definitely a cultural critique, Johnston's attack does not appear anchored to any specific social concern. This makes his amorphous tribute to absolute truth somewhat sinister, a non sequitur that leaves us wondering precisely what we have done to provoke it.

To me, a relativist attitude is simply recognition of the fact that perception shapes reality, that the same event can be seen differently by two people. Thus, relativism does not demand the staunch denial of some universal truth, but rather the acceptance that, due to limitations in language, perception, particle physics or whatever, this truth can never be wholly known to us. In other words, it's not offensive to suggest the existence of an ultimate reality; but it is wholly impudent to argue that you are actually in possession of this single truth, and are therefore authorized to squelch any dissenting views. Relativism does not allow the imposition of a single absolute view on everyone. This is a good thing.

If you believe in absolute truth, on the other hand, attaining an unimpeachable position is pretty straightforward. For instance, there's nothing to stop me from waking up tomorrow and proclaiming that I have divined the grand design of the universe, and every moral pronouncement I make shall henceforth be right and true. Of course, I'll have difficulty convincing anyone else to accept this view (unless it's couched in some seriously eloquent oration, perhaps peppered with bons mots). And that's the pesky thing about absolute truth. Everyone has their own idea what it should be.

Johnston argues that we should test such truth-claims against reality. This approach works well in science, since the facts of the natural world are generally immune to our perception of them, and therefore serve quite nicely as a criterion to evaluate truth. However, when reality can be influenced by our perceptions, this two-way interaction complicates matters and can render absolute truth meaningless. Consider the financial markets. The essence of investing is anticipating the future, but our expectations today can affect that future. As George Soros says, it is meaningless to speak of a true future value without buyers, sellers and a market, all of which contribute to a re-flexive reality that cannot exist without our biased perceptions.

From a social utilitarian standpoint, the epistemology of absolute truth is problematic. Historically, religious fanaticism has enabled and endorsed killing, crusades, inquisition and conversion; such adventures were fuelled primarily by the infallible righteousness of the perpetrators. Today, people worldwide condemn America's unilateral application of military power. Former Secretary of Defense Robert S. McNamara cautions that if we cannot convince like-minded nations of the merit of our case, we must re-examine our position. With this in mind, it's appalling to accuse the current administration of gratuitous relativism. After all, the president seems to speak almost exclusively in absolutes, eschewing any attempts at empathy towards "evildoers" who hate American freedom. After Sept. 11, Congress rallied together, united in support of war. On the eve of this landmark decision, dissenting views were discarded -- precisely when debate should be most vigorous. Ideological absolutism has no place in a democratic government.

Absolute truth also poses serious obstacles to free speech. After all, if we know the ultimate truth, why tolerate counterfactual or dissenting views? Many religions certainly don't. Any opinion that challenges accepted understanding is automatically heretical in such a system, so most inquiry must cease. The ongoing quest for truth is frozen by the premature adoption, ratification and fortification of convenient dogma. Not exactly the height of enlightenment.

Bizarrely, Johnston pronounces relativism inherently arrogant, because the opinion-holder "cannot be wrong." Relativism at least permits the existence of dissenting views, so to call this arrogant while excusing absolute truth is disingenuous. Perhaps the problem is not the views themselves, but the perceived equal treatment which they are afforded. I too criticize a philosophical paralysis wherein no single view can ever be favored over any other, though I daresay I prefer it to someone else's imposition of universal truth.

Absolute truth is unquestionably seductive. Surrender to it, and we can act with conviction, drunk on the nectar of a righteous God-given mission; we can pronounce laws without debate, safe in their unassailable validity. But if history teaches us anything in this regard, it is humility; after all, a staggering collection of once-unimpeachable beliefs turned out to be false.

To endorse one truth is the height of conceit. Echoing McNamara, good government demands empathy, not the righteous unilateralism of absolute truth.

My take:
Long live Guevara-sporting pre-frosh

April 28, 2005

L ast week, Keith Urbahn '06 lamented the three -- count them, three -- pre-frosh he spotted cavorting around this storied campus in politically incorrect left-leaning T-shirts ("Radical unchic: think before you wear," 4/20). The kids in question were here for Bulldog Days, eyeing Elis and weighing the merits of this fine institution. I sincerely hope these three students didn't happen upon that article, or otherwise catch this backhanded jab by the "unchained reactionary" himself; but in case they did, I offer an open letter to the three, Che Guevara-shirted pre-frosh:

Dear friends, you rock. You have earned the ire of the campus conservatives, always a top-shelf achievement, and you did it on your very first day.

Rest assured, young flock, your future classmates are not all sartorial snipers; nor, indeed, are the bulk of them shrill, unsavory witch-hunters. Speaking strictly from personal experience, polyester-sporting double-boiled Reaganites with "W" stickers and arcane prejudices are the exception at Yale, not the rule. And they're easily avoided: Just turn tail whenever you catch a whiff of "Donald Trump: The Fragrance."

(If Urbahn has license to build sweeping political generalizations on a smattering of T-shirts, surely he won't begrudge us a roast of the ultimate capitalist cologne.)

Fear not, pre-frosh, I see your Che Guevara shirts for what they are: a simple, pop-culture clothing selection with a fun, rebellious streak. I grant that you, tender academic tyros, may not yet know the complete story behind the Cuban Revolution. Nonetheless, I respect your freedom to wander around our daunting Ivy League campus sporting whatever logo you like. To assist you, I'll offer three bits of advice: Do resist the guilt-mongering that would make you ashamed of your contrarian political statements, do be prepared to defend your chosen logo, and do ward off raging campus conservatives, if you must.

Just so we're all on the same page, the fundamental concept of communism -- the one so revolting to narcissistic basket cases -- is equality. Yes, clashes did occur in those states that sought to implement this system, and yes, theorists did foresee these clashes in their writings. The imperfect implementation of Marx's concept is indeed to blame for a good number of ills; still, this hardly demands that Marxism "carried the seeds of mass murder within it," any more than Adam Smith is to be blamed for Ollie North hustling weapons to Iran. To brand a system of fundamental human equality as a recipe for ultimate evil is at once darkly humorous and dangerously misleading, since it tacitly exonerates capitalism, perhaps the single most damaging, exclusive, greed-fuelled system ever devised by man.

Now, before you send me your T-shirt, you ought to know: I'm quite at home in this capitalist society, but I'm not an apologist. I'll freely admit that this is a system that seems to particularly relish the exploitation of the poor, saddling them with crushing health bills and then yanking the rug out with corporate-lobbied bankruptcy reform. This is a system where hatred, intolerance and prejudice are rife, a system that has presided over some of the most brutal killing sprees in human history. American capitalism in particular maintains its dazed population in a spiraling eddy of revolving debt, fear and consumption, polluting, wasting and consuming resources at an alarming rate. Americans boast an environmental footprint of 25 acres per person; if everyone on Earth lived like an American, we'd need five planets just to sustain us. The point is simple -- you have good reason indeed for questioning the validity of this system, for it is your generation that will inherit its legacy.

Anyway, back to your Che shirt. While it is undoubtedly satisfying for Urbahn to smugly brand you mere "hipster poseurs," in doing so he trivializes your (potentially very earnest) opposition to the actions of the American government.

Don't mind the right-wingers; they'd prefer to mock the shirt you're wearing than change anything about the unjust world they occupy. And for pop-culture lessons, look elsewhere: perhaps to a college junior who doesn't put quotes around the word "cool."

I'm also prepared to concede that perhaps your T-shirt doesn't betray any political bias at all: Maybe you donned it seeking safe passage through the chanting throngs of GESO supporters who, like it or not, are a far more significant presence on campus than McCarthyist stooges and fashion police. Remember, for every "unchained reactionary" at Yale, there are dozens who would recoil with horror at a George W. Bush shirt, and, on the bright side, you did well to avoid irking them.

And to Mr. Urbahn, a suggestion: Lay off the pre-frosh. If you hope to target mindless drones ignorantly buying into the propaganda of wholesale slaughter, try looking closer to home. It's amazing what injustice is excused these days with the invocation of patriotism.

FOR HOUSING MARKET,
A CRAZE BELIES A CRISIS

SEPTEMBER 1, 2005

H urricane season notwithstanding, it's hard to watch
the news without seeing some report on the housing
market. And while real-estate investment never really
achieved broad collegiate appeal -- unlike keg stands,
for instance, or iPods -- this housing situation is nonetheless symp-
tomatic of, and contributing to, a debt crisis in America. Therefore,
to facilitate discussion on this important issue, I present my brief,
high-altitude summary of debt in America, and the three great delu-
sions of the housing fiasco.

First, a little context: On the tail of the dot-com crash, the Fed
lowered interest rates, hoping to avert recession with a soft landing.
The goal of this rate drop was to spur borrowing, quell saving and
inject money into the economy through consumer spending. The
9/11 attacks marked another impetus for economic slowdown, coun-
tered immediately with further rate cuts and those bizarre presidential edicts commanding citizens to travel to Disneyland and spend

money. This, in short, began a sustained, multi-year period of rock-bottom interest rates, which of course translated to cheaper borrowing costs, low mortgage rates and, among other things, more people eagerly shopping for homes.

A deluge of hungry buyers leads to market unbalance, and is met with increased production where feasible, and increased prices where not. This is exactly what occurred in some coastal markets of California, Florida and the Northeast, with home prices soaring alongside a boom in new development wherever space would permit. In the hottest markets -- like Los Angeles, San Diego and Miami -- house prices have posted double-digit annual appreciation for several years, with many properties doubling or trebling in value since 2002.

The exact definition of a speculative bubble is the subject of some debate, but, for our purposes, let's say it constitutes any situation where people feel compelled to invest with urgency in a product whose intrinsic value is less important than the promise of profit. Thus, the nature of the product and the price paid are functionally irrelevant, as long as some buyer exists who is willing to pay even more. This "greater fool" theory powered the recent dot-com boom, just as it once fuelled the Dutch tulip craze.

This brings us to Delusion One: that real estate always rises in value. Any cursory study of history will show this belief is simply untrue; nonetheless, polls show that a disturbing number of people believes real estate values always go up. A significant share of homes is now sold to speculators (or "flippers"), whose only intent is to re-sell the property for profit.

That real estate can only increase in value is a dangerous assumption, one that bears primary responsibility for Delusion Two: that negative-amortization, interest-only mortgages are a good idea. If home prices in your area have outstripped the amount you can afford, you might weigh what Alan Greenspan politely termed an "exotic mortgage": a debt where, despite hefty monthly payments, you are left after five years owing more on your house than its initial sale price. Without getting mired in detail, such mortgages defer all principal and some interest payments for a set period, usually two to five years, end-loading the unpaid interest onto the principal. In my view, such products are useful in only two instances: first, when a buyer's income will increase sufficiently to cover the major jump in payments after the five-year introductory period; and second, if the property value will rise sufficiently during those five years to cover the increased principal with a sale. If either of these assumptions proves untrue, the owner is in trouble. Unheard-of as recently as 2001, in some areas such mortgages are now used in upwards of three-quarters of all home purchases.

And here we introduce the important -- if obvious -- notion that in order to profit from real-estate appreciation, you must actually sell your property. The problem with this is that, unless you rent or move to a different city -- or the property in question is a second house -- any comparable house you can buy is just as pricey as the one you're selling. This unfortunate complication has been termed the "golden prison" phenomenon: Homeowners watch helplessly as their houses appreciate, unable to cash in without spending even more to move.

This quandary is nicely sidestepped by a wholehearted immersion in Delusion Three: borrowing against inflated home equity realizes your gains. Overheated markets have produced outlandish home prices, prices that utterly outstrip the ability of the average household to afford modest dwellings with any but the most exotic debt instruments. Borrowing against such inflated appraisals isn't realizing gains ? it's staking money on those valuations. Nonetheless, home equity loans have injected significant cash into the economy in recent years;

much consumer spending is therefore fuelled on borrowed money secured by overvalued assets ? hardly the hallmark of a robust financial system.

American indebtedness has reached epidemic proportions. Greenspan deferred a deserved recession with a sustained infusion of cheap money, allowing us to deny reality for a few years. But amid this furor of consumption, warning signs abound: The personal savings rate dropped to zero in June. Foreclosures and bankruptcies are up, the latter at record highs. Check-cashing joints are among the fastest growing businesses in the nation -- a glaring beacon of a society living above its means. The housing bubble looks poised to burst: Rents remain low, often falling far short of covering the mortgage costs on rapidly appreciating properties, and in many markets housing may already have peaked -- evidenced by a drought of buyers amid a glut of stale listings.

Across the country, millions cling to the belief that housing gains are real, hoping their prime store of wealth won't suddenly evaporate in a market correction. And who knows? Maybe they're right. Maybe interest rates will stay at record lows, home prices will continue to appreciate, and an insatiable pack of well-heeled suckers will buy anything that needs to sell. Too many homeowners are staking everything on the best possible scenario, praying that a rainy day will never come.

We all hope for the best -- but don't bet the house on it.

WAL-MART DEAL WITH GAYS
SPARKS EVANGELICAL IRE

NOVEMBER 16, 2006

This holiday season, Wal-Mart faces a boycott. To most Yalies, this is hardly controversial: Our idealistic ivory-tower classmates are rarely enchanted with union-busting, health-care-withholding corporate mega-chains. But this latest criticism comes not from liberal activists, but from evangelical Christians. Their complaint? Wal-Mart is cooperating with homosexuals to further the "gay agenda."

On Aug. 21, the National Gay and Lesbian Chamber of Commerce announced that the world's largest retailer had joined a long list of corporate partners, all pledging to include LGBT-owned businesses on their supply radar. Evidently anxious about the response in the Bible belt, Wal-Mart kept the deal quiet and let the NLGCC announce the partnership. A sneaky move, but insufficient to evade the alert snouts of anti-gay Christian watchdogs.

The most vocal of these is Don Wildmon, chairman of the American Family Association. This group launched an e-mail campaign, spamming 3 million supporters and urging a boycott on holiday shopping at Wal-Mart. The company should be punished, apparently, for daring to suggest that the "homosexual agenda" is worthy of support.

What precisely is the "homosexual agenda?"

Judging by most gay people I know, I'd say their only real "agenda" is to live a normal life, and perhaps escape persecution by spiteful bigots. I sense this is not the agenda to which Wildmon refers.

So what is it? According to a sinister book titled "The Gay Agenda" by Pastor Ronnie Floyd, the problem is that homosexuality threatens the "traditional family." Our families are under attack, he suggests, and a return to a traditional family values - with attendant far-right ideological baggage, of course - will set society right.

What rubbish. Even if we arbitrarily anoint the "traditional family" as ideal, it's still unclear how the presence of homosexuals in society threatens any individual instance of it. Such a premise depends upon a delirious and totally fictitious characterization of gays as depraved, Constitution-shredding bogeymen with a diet rich in moral fiber. If roving gangs of homosexuals stalked the land devouring families, I might sympathize.

They don't. I can't. Back to Wal-Mart.

In hopes of comprehending the boycotters' anger, I queried the issue online. A rash of hits led to the popular conservative news site "WorldNetDaily," whose intensive coverage of this matter (which ran alongside articles titled "Mommy, there's a liberal under my bed" and "Corporate America snuggles up to gays") includes the story of Janet Baird, a longtime Wal-Mart employee.

Janet worked at Wal-Mart for 14 years, a job she described as "a ministry given to me by God Himself to help His people in need." She quit instantly when she learned the company was negotiating with homosexuals, and overnight began picketing her Ohio store entrance and urging a boycott. She described this activity as bringing "the Gospel of Christ to the very gates of Hell." Her stance? Sam Walton "loved God," but "the store he began does not."

So, to clarify: A company agrees to consider goods produced by gay-run businesses, and suddenly it's transformed from God's ministry into the seat of Satan. Both seem like strong reactions to a retail outlet. Of course, I was also unaware that big-box stores were capable of loving God. I have much to learn.

In the wild eyes of fanatical Bible-thumpers, dealing with homosexuals is Wal-Mart's third misstep this year. First, the company neglected to acknowledge Christmas in its catalog, referring instead only to a nondescript "Holiday" season. This predictably whipped Christian activists to a fury. Next, the store agreed to sell "Brokeback Mountain" on DVD. That heartwarming tale of two strapping ranchers finding love in a rain-pattered tent evidently hit too close to home for heartland tough-guys and drew heavy fire as well. The store recently buckled and returned "Christmas" to its vocabulary, but on the other two has thus far stood firm.

The Wal-Mart-NGLCC partnership isn't about God, Hell or preserving the family; it's about money. Facing waning sales, the company hoped to boost its customer base and combat its stigma in the gay community. They have done this before, partnering with Hispanic and other groups in hopes of fostering a community-friendly image. Usually, no one much cares.

But given the furious backlash from their bedrock Christian clientele, one does wonder why they don't just renege. After all, it's unlikely that the gay community - traditionally liberal and thus hardly enamored with Wal-Mart on any front - will suddenly embrace the chain, and if Don Wildmon and his wild minions succeed, the company could take a major financial hit. It will be interesting to see what happens after Thanksgiving, when the boycott officially kicks in.

The evangelical right continues to rejoice in backward parochialism and institutionalized bigotry. The need to satisfy their interests imposes sharp constraints on political parties and businesses alike. That the world's largest retailer has stood up to this so far is encouraging.

Let's hope it lasts.

FEWER GUNS WOULD HELP STOP FUTURE TRAGEDIES

APRIL 19, 2007

Monday's mass murder at Virginia Tech was the worst shooting rampage in American history. As the investigation continues and details of the crime continue to emerge, we strain to comprehend what drove Tech senior Cho Seung-Hui to slaughter so many of his peers — and we face hard questions about how to prevent such eruptions in the future.

Tuesday morning, I was returning to New Haven from a weekend in Washington, D.C. As I drove, my car radio picked up a succession of local stations, sampling in series many early reactions to the tragedy. DJs and talk radio hosts of all political stripes grappled with the same awful information, salvaging facts from the mess to shore up familiar positions. As for what lesson to take from the killings, everyone, it seemed, had a different view.

Some blamed Tech president Charles Steger for mishandling the unfolding tragedy, and demanded his resignation — but university presidents are not selected on the basis of their comfort with violent crime, and this is as it should be. Others accused the campus police, claiming they fumbled the initial double homicide by failing to notify students immediately of the missing shooter. That issue is beyond the ambit of pundits (or columnists) to decide, though it will surely be vigorously debated in the weeks to come.

Everyone agreed on a need for societal response, to assure us that such a tragedy will not be repeated. But what can universities really do to prevent a recurrence? The best anyone could come up with was air-raid sirens on campus, and a plan to text-message students in an emergency — neither of which would have helped those already trapped in Norris Hall. In this case, Cho Seung-Hui alerted authorities early with the dormitory murders; but whether or not we believe police squandered that lead, we surely cannot count on such foreshadowing again. Thus, we are left with the grim reality that a determined gunman is free to strike virtually at will, leaving police to react much as they did on Monday.

A more proactive idea was pitched as I drove past Philadelphia. That commentator argued ardently and in apparent seriousness that what campus police really need is shoulder-fired rifles, to neutralize students at 60-plus yards. Faced with a madman brandishing two pistols, it is conceptually satisfying to engage in this form of hypothetical arms race, arming the good guys with superior firepower; but what of a killer with automatic weapons? Surely we should equip Yale Security with bazookas, just in case.

More seductive in these heightened circumstances is one commentator's contention that, had every student in the building been packing a pistol, Cho's rampage could have been aborted. Granted, this is perhaps true, and if slaughter were an everyday occurrence at colleges, we might do well to outfit students like soldiers. However, rational minds will recognize that arming college students is unlikely to increase campus safety — rather, it is likely to precipitate shootouts where none would otherwise occur.

Moreover, that entire premise hinges upon good, law-abiding citizens carrying weapons to combat "evil" criminals. The former sail through background checks and purchase their firearms legally; the latter are lifelong scum and obtain their guns through illicit means. Notwithstanding the false dichotomy of this conception, we must remember that until this week, Cho Seung-Hui belonged to the first group: His guns were legally bought, his record clean.

We have heard, these past few days, of the countless warnings this deranged proto-criminal shed like chaff around campus. The fact that a student with a demonstrated history of harassment, depression, extreme antisocial behavior and unspeakably disturbed writings nonetheless aced a Virginia background check should speak for itself. To those who champion current gun laws, we need no further rebuttal.

Despite all efforts, society has proven largely unsuccessful at defusing ticking time bombs like Cho; it is evidently impossible to identify or corral potentially dangerous individuals with any consistency. It makes sense, then, to reduce their eventual impact by complicating the acquisition of firearms.

America might begin by following the lead of other nations faced with similar tragedies.

In a 1996 school shooting in Dunblane, Scotland, an ex-scout leader armed with four legally owned pistols killed 16 primary school children and their teacher. A petition led by parents secured several hundred thousand signatures and successfully lobbied the Conservative government into banning handguns in the U.K. Anyone caught with one today faces five years in prison.

Just weeks after the Dunblane massacre, an unemployed man

shot and killed 35 tourists in Port Arthur, Australia. This too spurred significant government action, virtually outlawing assault rifles and instating strict limits on gun ownership. Similar restrictions are commonplace worldwide.

Over 40,000 people die each year from gunshot wounds in the United States. Per capita, this is nearly five times more than Australia, and a staggering 34 times more than the U.K.

But those who characterize shooting sprees as uniquely American are only half correct: As these examples demonstrate, no nation is immune from gun violence, but smart governments react swiftly to prevent such tragedies from occurring again.

The right to bear arms is a cherished American liberty, anchored in a fairly recent constitutional interpretation and bolstered by a powerful gun lobby. Periodic slaughter may well be the price of such liberty. If so, Americans should retire these perceived freedoms and with them, their increasing, awful and heart-rending cost.

If only this most recent tragedy were enough.

Technology

A DIGITAL LEXICON
THAT'S ENGLISH GONE WRONG

FEBRUARY 15, 2005

As a bioinformatics scientist, programmer and sometime Internet-security wannabe, I am regularly inundated with tech vernacular. The time has come, in my view, for a great airing of dirty laundry. My complaint: the sad state in which the digital age has left our mother tongue.

I write here not to condemn the endless acronyms, chat-room lingo or obscure scripting code, nor even to rant against the all-prevalent i-, e-, My- and Cyber- prefixes. Rather, I am struck by the prevalence of "tech" language, and the way this has shaped and distorted our everyday vocabulary. In my naive attempt to taxonomize this phenomenon, I have roughly delineated three distinct categories of offense: Repurposing, Senseless Juxtaposition and Imaginary Rubbish.

Repurposing concerns those otherwise normal English words now sneakily imbued with new meaning. In a mere two decades, a cadre of Jolt-swilling dorks has corrupted countless old favorites, yielding limping, sulking, chimeric portmanteaus. Many useful words have thusly wandered astray. Virus. Surfing. Firewall. Buffer. Icon. Meet the Death Row inmates of portmanteau prison. All these specimens had an active life before being pressed into service to tag increasingly trivial flotsam from the digital age. Pity them, as you might ache for the Dodo bird or $2 movie rentals. All, sadly, are lost.

Trademarked names are another bastion of corruption: the native meanings of words like Windows, Apache, Amazon, Office, Yahoo and Outlook are all but vanquished by their copyrighted squatters, and Apple is working hard to do the same with Safari. While on the subject, Apple itself is a prime offender, and generator of such droll spin-offs as AppleTalk, Apple key and AppleShare. (At least the latter sounds like a directive for selfish preschoolers; the others stray quickly into the territory of absinthe-fueled hallucination). Not to play favorites, Microsoft has dealt out some winners too: Desktop Explorer is among my favorites, invoking images of diminutive, handlebar-sporting Brits in pith helmets leading an expedition to tame the wild jungle of some cluttered oaken writing surface. "Jolly good, old chap! Let's go desktop exploring! Right-o, it's a veritable safari, old boy!" Pardon me, Safari (TM). And yes, thanks to BlackBerry, even fruits are fair game.

The silver lining to this fiasco is found in the second category, *Senseless Juxtaposition*, where we realize that the vast re-badging effort can produce some true comedic gold by incongruous pairing of altered terms. Personal favorites include such odd marriages as "token ring," "memory stick," "Palm Pilot," "millennium bug" and "warm boot"; perhaps equally rich are peculiar directives such as "insert table," "drag and drop," "publish to web," "expand tree" and "delete cookies." But even these bow down to the priceless "packet sniffer." Use it sparingly: It is a true titan of absurd coupling.

And thus, we arrive at *Imaginary Rubbish*. While the preceding

terms are repurposed versions of pre-existing words -- and therefore lend themselves to ironic double-entendres -- an entire genus
of the tech lexicon comprises nutty, unreal words that are entirely
and wholly fabricated. The online emissions of the young and tech-
savvy now read like a modern-day Jabberwocky, replete with imaginary terms like "dongle," "Google" and "podcast." Poor Lewis Carroll
would pass out reading PC World. Among these vast untamed rushes
of nonsense, it's hard to pick a favorite, but nonetheless a few pockets
of mystery stand out. Why, for instance, must processors sport names
suitable for Transformers, or 60s-era robots? "I am Athlon, son of
Opteron and Pentium. I come to Google."

Despite all this silliness, the drive to expand, change and reshape
our language is an almost unstoppable force; both the re-minting
of established words and the frantic generation of new ones highlights the frenetic pace of the technological boom that surrounds us.
Striving to tag abstract concepts, those on the frontiers of the digital
advance continue to pillage our vocabulary; dictionaries struggle to
maintain authority athwart the rogue waves of new words, their editors snap-judging the terms pounding against their gates and hastily
endorsing those that blast right past them into common usage.

Those who seek to oppose such redefinition ultimately face a losing
battle: Consider the contested definition of "hacker," which techies
have long insisted refers only to those who deeply enjoy poring over
minutiae, or hacking away at assembler-level code. As TechWeb la-
ments, "the term [hacker] has unfortunately become synonymous in
the popular press with 'cracker,' a person who performs an illegal act.
This use of the term is not appreciated by the overwhelming majority
of hackers who are honest professionals." Good luck, TechWeb, considering that every major news outlet in the country favors "hacker"
for malicious usage.

Care to witness a pointless battle against popular opinion? Watch this space.

So next time you boot Windows on your notebook -- whether to rip, burn, surf, chat, download or check webmail -- remember that what you just read was gibberish 20 years ago. We might not even recognize the English of tomorrow, but for now at least, let's all say "huzzah!" for Google, dongles and packet sniffers.

LET BLOGGER BEWARE:
WEB PROSE TRAVELS FAR

MARCH 30, 2006

I've had it with blog users and their double standard of personal privacy. The reasoning goes like this: Bloggers are free to choke the Internet with drivel and pepper their tedious memoirs with keywords that ensnare innocent Google users. But if a stranger should stumble upon their blogs and actually read what they have published, this "trespasser" stands accused of invading their privacy.

This happens more than you might think. On one blog I used to read, the author proudly declared that an abundance of law school fee waivers had allowed her to buy a $500 pair of shoes. When some uninvited reader commented that such behavior perverted the intent of fee waivers, she freaked out, squealed about shattered privacy and deleted her entire blog.

Granted, such drastic response is rare. Most bloggers won't obliterate their whole corpus of writing at the first negative comment. But they will vigorously protest any intrusion into their digital fiefdom. As though publishing the minute-by-minute trivia of their lives to the Internet is not arrogance enough, the rest of us must now face condemnation if we so much as stumble upon their pages.

I think the problem stems from a false impression of online privacy. In the beginning, the nascent blog is blissfully sheltered. Visitors are always friends or family; search engine lag, luck and the small amount of searchable text ensure that newbie bloggers are well-insulated from random traffic. At ease, they begin to take this veneer of privacy for granted -- until one day, they awake to find the facade toppled, the door ajar and some Google-fed interloper rummaging through their holiday snaps. The ambushed blogger then circles the wagons, expels the defiler with an IP ban and bewails the rape of their fictitious solitude. Alas, such is life on the Internet. Swim at your own risk.

Among writers, bloggers are unique in feeling violated when a stranger reads what they publish. As a columnist, I accept that my work may be read by friends, strangers, enemies or no one at all; I can't imagine a writer who, when his work is mentioned, shrieks that you shouldn't have read it in the first place. We columnists may be self-important know-it-alls, but at least we don't sully our rhetorical exhibitionism with retroactive invocations of ersatz privacy. Columnists 1, Bloggers 0.

I've heard blogging dismissed as mere online journalizing, with the concomitant suggestion that we should treat random blogs as private diaries and resist the urge to peek. This is pure confusion. A journal is a private written record of personal affairs and thoughts. It doesn't matter whether you scribble nightly confessions in a leatherbound tome or bang them out in Microsoft Word; a diary is a diary. The line is crossed when you publish this material, and the attention of others is sought. A journal is a favor to oneself; a blog is foisted upon an undeserving public, also as a favor to oneself.

Of course, if blogs were truly a clearinghouse for diary-grade secrets, they would be more riveting. Sadly, most people are too shy or decorous to divulge sensitive emotional matter online. Their blogs suffer, emerging piecemeal as an unfortunate, declawed half-breed, devoid of anything juicy and freighted instead with petulant whining, self-important proselytizing and some of the most mundane confessions ever recorded. "My latte burned my tongue!" Someone call CNN.

True, not all blogging is so insipid. Just yesterday I enjoyed a first-hand account of a woman's struggle to return lip gloss to an uncooperative cashier. The gee-whiz tale soon deteriorated into a seething condemnation of union labor that would make a Walton blush. I'm sure sliding a soapbox under every cranky citizen was a fabulous idea in principle. In reality, pairing belligerent grannies with split-second publishing and a complete lack of accountability doesn't inspire civil discourse. Just think, acrimonious narcissists can now throw tantrums for the entire world. Bully for us.

And let's not forget the derivative punditry and TrackBack orgies of political bloggers. After all, where else can you watch a closed system of fame-seeking, blazer-sporting youth bicker incessantly, shamelessly quote themselves and steal visitors from each other's blogs? The result is like some nightmarish book-signing gala, where everyone in attendance thinks he's the star author.

All told, I'm not too impressed by the so-called blog revolution. The experts promised remarkable things, like the infusion of fresh blood into grass-roots democratic action or the emergence of some grand literary-political salon. The end result, to me, looks more like a million cynical monkeys typing out complaint letters and cramming them in our collective suggestion box -- then hissing furiously when we deign to read them.

Bloggers, it's time to accept that publishing online means inviting a world of window-shoppers to your personal bazaar of bad grammar and unchecked neuroses. You can't have it both ways. If you can't stand the thought of strangers perusing your writing, maybe it doesn't belong on something named the "World Wide Web."

That's one yellow card for the bloggers. Play on.

A PECULIAR AFTERLIFE, COURTESY OF THE WEB

OCTOBER 13, 2005

With Halloween around the corner, it's time to get a jump on Internet haunting. I'm not talking about ghosts posting on message boards or mysterious noises in your hard drive. No, Internet haunting is a real phenomenon, though it's perhaps not quite what you think.

Today, most students cast a significant and growing online shadow. We flood the world with e-mails. We post our profiles on the Facebook, Friendster or MySpace. We dither away the hours chatting through instant messengers. We keep blogs, maintain personal Web sites, share photos online, text each other all day and post grammatical train wrecks on discussion boards. And one day, we die.

So what happens to these online identities when we shuffle off this mortal coil? For a rare few individuals with extraordinary foresight, passwords are saved, records are kept and the task of dismantling their online existence falls to a relative. But for the vast majority of us, we live on. We haunt.

This sobering thought is apparently outside the ambit of acceptable party conversation. When I broached the topic at a barbeque last weekend, I was met with shocked silence. After a pause, one fellow asked me, jaw agape, "You ? you've got dead Friendsters?" No, in fact, I do not. But I will someday, as will you. As flesh-and-blood humans, our ultimate mortality needs hardly to be driven home, but the digital world we inhabit is all too good at preserving exactly the impressions we make.

The stuff we post to the Internet can have a staggeringly long half-life. A grad school colleague recently uncovered an online personal ad from a professor we both know, dating back to the mid-90s. It was preserved and dutifully indexed by Google Groups. I'm guessing our would-be Romeo wouldn't have hit "submit" so fast had he foreseen his own students chuckling a decade later. (To make matters worse, 10 long years yielded not one reply to his ad.)

This little anecdote emphasizes the surprising longevity of even our most casual online emissions. So yes, your own past can haunt you. But worse still, if you're not careful, your entire digital present could linger on to haunt everyone else, forever.

In our society, it's customary to speak well of the departed. Over the past few years, I've noticed that when a friend passes away, our instinct as students is apparently to visit their profile and pay homage by eulogizing in the testimonials area. This makes for some awkward maneuvering as we, suddenly somber, try to ignore our own earlier, teasing messages still staring up from the screen. Worse yet, while we wax lyrical about the merits of the deceased, we do so mere pixels below their now-irrevocable keg-stand photo, or a transcribed drunk-text they'd surely rather forget. One has to wince.

You'd think someone would have dealt with this -- after all, people die all the time -- and to some extent, they have. Friendster has an official policy wherein deceased members' profiles can be converted to memorial pages. However, since this process requires that the user -- presumably someone in possession of his password, not the deceased himself -- log in and make it so, to date only a handful of people have actually exercised this option.

Leaning toward the macabre, a Web site titled MyLastEmail.com offers a service wherein, in exchange for an annual fee, five e-mails are stored and then released to loved ones upon your death. I'm not entirely sure what this is supposed to accomplish, since you could just as easily store such missives in hardcopy with a will; admittedly, your death-memos would then no longer arrive with a banner offering low-rate mortgage refinancing or enticing challenges to click the monkey and win an iPod. And seriously, if grandma can click that monkey through her tears, that alone is worth 30 bucks a year.

Is there a better solution? Rather than timidly releasing death e-mails from beyond the grave -- a practice more likely to terrify than soothe the recipient -- I hereby propose a posthumous legacy-scrubber. Like Victor the Cleaner in La Femme Nikita, this company could sanitize all your profiles, render them family-safe, and whitewash those pesky testimonials. We'll post death notices to all your favorite message boards, retire your blog and put your best possible picture back on the Facebook. Shell out for our premium service, and we also promise not to spam people from your messenger account when you're dead. It's a pretty good deal, all told.

Fine, premature death is no place to turn a profit. But, all kidding aside, this really is an issue where an ounce of prevention can mean six feet of cure. I'm not suggesting we post solemn eulogies as Facebook profiles, or indeed live life as some morbid trudge toward our final day. But we might give some thought to storing our account information someplace, perhaps with instructions to address the most glaringly gauche beacons of our online existence. Otherwise, those compromising photos and inside jokes we deposit on Facebook may well be our digital legacy. And that, my friends, is just poor form.

IN-FLIGHT NUISANCES
BRING TRAVEL TO NEW LOW

APRIL 13, 2006

Early this morning, as I was trying to sleep on a flight, it struck me that air travel is no fun anymore. Flying today is worse than unremarkable. It's downright depressing.

In its early days, commercial flight was chic and exclusive: the idle rich jet-setting around the globe, prim stewardesses in pillbox hats. But though the ritziness has vanished, airline travel has retained an idiosyncratic collection of characteristic peculiarities.

Until recently, the airline experience was pretty constant. Passengers enjoyed demurely packaged meals of infamously poor quality ? free with airfare ? and tiny bottles of liquor, also gratis. The in-flight movie played on a single screen, with funny beige earphones piping hollow soundtrack from the armrest. A soft "ding" accompanied the "Fasten seatbelt" warning.

Uniformed flight crew gestured at exits, dangled yellow oxygen masks and donned flotation devices in the aisles. Ah, those were the halcyon flights of our youth.

Today, food costs extra. The safety demo is pre-recorded. The movie shows on dozens of tiny screens, and you can't hear it without shelling out five bucks for a junk headset. And the "Fasten seatbelt" sign now has no functional purpose; like its "No smoking" cousin, it's simply always on.

But beyond these changes lies something far more sinister: the encroaching of our growth-crazed consumerist mindset into the once-sacred aisles of the jetliner.

This struck me as we reached cruising altitude. Releasing my tray table, I was dismayed to find its surface rudely clad in a gaudy Verizon ad.

Since when have companies taken to advertising on my dinner tray? Worse, since every tray-table in the aircraft bore identical advertisements, mealtime was a kaleidoscopic cacophony of inappropriate marketing; I felt rather like a fly, if my compound eye could see only Verizon logos and Cobb salads.

The experience, while farcical, seemed oddly demeaning. Successful advertising should preserve at least the illusion of choice. Whether we are paging through a glossy magazine, flipping channels or even glancing at a billboard, our attention should be courted, not coerced. Nowadays, advertisements are crammed in our faces at inopportune times: while urinating, for instance, or while pecking at an airline meal. I prefer not to be counseled while on the toilet, especially in matters as trivial as which chewing gum to buy. A similar advertising blackout extends to dinner time. Consequently, I shall make it a point not to buy any Verizon products this week, on account of that company's evident willingness to harass a seatbelted audience already burdened with day-old salads and swollen feet.

A further intrusion is the SkyMall catalog. You can find this unwelcome development crammed in your seat pocket, cozying up to the airsick bag. SkyMall is a thick, glossy catalog now found on major airlines. It offers the most peculiar collection of merchandise: an array of goods so wholly absurd that the only way to replicate it would surely involve Philip K. Dick, Lewis Carroll and a barrel of ether.

Why not invest in the ludicrous "PoshAir Cocoon"? It's a "modern, hygienic sleeping accommodation" that looks strikingly like a flannel condom with armholes. At last, you can zip yourself into comfort, and broadcast your status as a xenophobic, germophobic, spendthrift idiot to an entire airplane of snickering people. Or perhaps you'd prefer a stuffed dog toy with a camera hidden in the nose. (I dare not dream what combination of preschool-aged children and illicit spying begat this creepy hybrid.) And that's not all.

Marvel at the raw utilitarian brawn of the "Solar Powered Mole Repeller" on page 70. I have no idea whether moles plague my garden, but this device will set things right. The vibrating post "drives them crazy," since moles "just cannot tolerate that underground vibration!" But perhaps my favorite item is the in-ground swimming pool on page 109. For $19,400, you can order your very own, and you can do so from 35,000 feet.

This is, quite simply, the most ridiculous in-flight catalog imaginable. Buying these items on the ground would be bad enough, but the need to acquire them at cruising altitude is completely beyond comprehension. Has anyone actually bought a $70 "feline drinking fountain" during the in-flight movie? Actually, never mind. I don't want to know.

Alas, apparently, this is progress. Traveling by air was once a special experience. Now, sadly, it shares a great deal with visiting a public restroom: It's institutional, unpleasant and overrun by ads. Occasionally unavoidable, it must simply be endured.

Why have airplanes become a mail-order mall in the sky? Perhaps a cabin pressurized at 5,000 feet predisposes a planeload of suckers to buying $20,000 swimming pools.

Or maybe air travel merely reflects broader problems in our society. If so, the subtle decay of character, the encroachment of advertising and the general commercial sleaziness on board are cause for concern.

'INTELLIPEDIA'?
CIA JUMPS ON WIKI WAGON

NOVEMBER 2, 2006

O n Tuesday, with Washington still fighting a Foley Internet hangover, the news wires reported that the U.S. intelligence community is using Intellipedia, a sort of top-secret wiki for spies and Feds. Aimed at improving inter-agency collaboration, the system was launched in April and now boasts over 3,600 users and 28,000 (highly classified) articles. But can a dash of Web 2.0 zeitgeist fix the intelligence business?

At a basic level, the new system makes sense. With 16 different agencies, shared goals and many areas of overlap, the intelligence community could likely profit from a comprehensive, communally updated information depository. Ideally, such a system would automate information collation and offer a pre-synthesized crock pot of high-test tattle. Preparing the National Intelligence Estimate would then become simply a matter of bulk-dumping the wiki's contents to a file and whisking it to the president.

Moreover, thanks to that pesky Iraq WMD snafu, collaboration is very much in vogue. Any resource that purports to blend the input of multiple agencies - and thereby disperse blame across a suitably wide area - will be greeted with enthusiasm. Prima facie, then, Intellipedia seems like a unifying breath of fresh air for an enterprise long mired in bureaucratic tangles and red tape.

But is it? Consider its public twin, Wikipedia.

Wikipedia is a popular online encyclopedia open to revision by users worldwide. Anyone can open an account, and then create or edit articles. The site is a tremendous resource, though by nature it is never guaranteed authoritative. Because any user can edit another's work, the words of a pre-eminent particle physics scholar, for instance, can in principle be freely modified by a bleary-eyed freshman on his third all-nighter. The most recent revision will stick.

Despite this apparent limitation, most Wikipedia articles are surprisingly robust. Malicious edits and fakery do occur, but users largely police themselves. Moderators delete bogus content and retire irrelevant pages, and most troublemakers can't be bothered to corrupt random articles that their peers will never see anyway. The site succeeds because the majority of users publish the truth.

In the intelligence business, however, ample motive exists to tweak reality.

Consider the intense focus on Iraq in the wake of the Sept. 11, 2001, terrorist attacks. Swapping the amorphous target of scattered cave-bound Islamic terrorists for an expedient scapegoat in Saddam Hussein would be unthinkable without solid evidence cementing their connection. Tasked with uncovering such a link, the intelligence community went to work. The result? A nation that had not collaborated with bin Laden nonetheless became the target of a major retaliatory war.

Presumably, an unbiased and cautious assessment of the facts would have mirrored the ultimate finding of the Sept. 11 commission in June 2004, which flatly rejected any link between Iraq and al-Qaida. And surely some honest analysts protested the initial findings but were silenced or sidelined to preserve the cause at hand.

Given this climate, I doubt Intellipedia will nurture or reward dissenting voices within the intelligence establishment anytime soon. If it doesn't, we've just affixed a multi-agency rubber stamp to the work of the same warmongering misinformation artists who designed and implemented the Iraq war. Jolly good.

Even if we are satisfied with the motives of intelligence staff, the Intellipedia system still raises security concerns. Is it wise to publish sensitive documents en masse to a digital network, and then make them available to thousands of workers from assorted agencies?

The Transportation Security Authority and national laboratories can now access Intellipedia. There is talk of inviting Britain, Canada and Australia to contribute, and even of granting access to China, allegedly so doctors there can comment on avian flu. All this seems like a recipe for trouble. Then again, I've always secretly hoped to see airport baggage handlers and rural Chinese doctors weigh in on American strategic defense policy, so why not? Let the media leaks begin.

Interestingly, Intellipedia is just one facet of the intelligence community's proud foray into the world of Web-based diversion. Eric Haseltine, chief scientist for the Director of National Intelligence, recently bragged: "We are using wikis, we are using blogs, we are using chat, we are using instant messaging." Impressive haul, Eric: the Four Horsemen of Internet time-wasting, right there. Just add Facebook and you'll have a full house. (How about a Mini-Feed for Gitmo inmates? You know, "The warden was tagged in a photo," or "Prisoner X27 wrote on his wall.")

The Feds are amassing a suite of procrastination tools that would make any high-schooler jealous. It is gratifying to note that Mark Foley's very public loss to instant messenger-fueled temptation last month seemingly has not curbed government enthusiasm for fun Internet distraction.

In a sense, Intellipedia is a sobering reminder of just how ho-hum the intelligence community really is. We glamorize the business: Spies are patriotic charmers with high-tech gadgets, and analysts are devoted and omniscient eggheads with advanced computers and top-secret software. It's deflating, then, when the CIA squeals over publicly available open-source hand-me-downs like a child on Christmas morning. Yeah, wikis are cool. We know. We use them.

Sigh. Does this mean there's no laser watch?

'SECOND LIFE' NOT READY
TO REPLACE FIRST

OCTOBER 19, 2006

On Tuesday, Reuters assigned a full-time reporter to cover a virtual-reality environment called Second Life. The news agency will now bring breaking headlines to thousands of immersed characters, and perhaps more interesting, pipe game-world news to our real-world Web. So what is this virtual playground?

According to its Web site, Second Life (SL) is an "online society within a 3D world, where users can explore, build, socialize, and participate in their own economy." It has amassed nearly a million members since opening in 2003. People sign in, design avatars, wander around and most importantly, spend money. They own land and do business. Toyota, Sony, Adidas and Starwood Hotels have all established digital outposts there. While access to the world itself is free, SL has a thriving, $130 million (U.S.) per year economy built upon "Linden Dollars." (Current exchange rate: L$ 273 to $1 U.S.)

Admittedly, this all sounds pretty interesting. Attempts to create viable virtual-reality cultures have in past been bogged down by crushingly slow frame-rates, sparse and irregular attendance, and a limited set of available actions. At first glance, SL seems to sidestep these problems. It boasts massive membership, apparently addictive interaction and broadband-supported animation. Moreover, the world is almost entirely user-created. People design their own buildings, items and clothing; those with marketable skills can sell their work to others; and so on.

Provide the framework, and let users supply the content: the Web 2.0 model. This approach has worked wonders for Flickr, Blogger and MySpace. Can it save virtual reality?

I joined SL to find out. I downloaded the software, logged in and was deposited onto "Orientation Island" with the other neophytes. I "edited my appearance" until satisfied with my ensemble: pompadour, beard, zebra-print skirt and thick leather vest. After a brief and fruitless attempt to make small talk with a mostly-nude female (note: virtual world thus far eerily real), I found the exit and teleported to the main game area.

It is difficult to describe the scene that awaited me. I arrived at an open, wooden structure atop a grassy hill with perhaps two dozen characters milling around inside. Three well-rendered exotic dancers gyrated amidst a crush of males; a black-clad gentleman was flying (literally, flying) in tight circles above the women, while a lanky blue-haired nudist tore around the room shouting obscenities that would make Mark Foley blush. A tiny female named Cherry - according to the nameplate floating above her head - was strangely clad in a browser texture, her entire body a shrink-wrapped Facebook screenshot. She was addressing the room in general, complaining that she couldn't "find the right menu." Mr. Blue Hair made her an offer entirely unfit for print.

As extraordinary as I found it, this wild scrum was evidently commonplace: The Reuters newshound was nowhere to be seen.

So this was Second Life, the future of e-commerce. The sober description I'd seen online seemed ill suited to the mad whirl before me.

Focus. $130 million per year, you say? All right, I can handle it. Let's talk turkey.

I entered the fray, and asked where to buy some Adidas, or a Toyota. A male character in nightclub attire shouted, "Who wants to ROCK?" and immediately broke out some dance moves. A bikini-clad female approached me and a menu popped up, inviting me to do various X-rated things. ("Buy a Toyota" was not on the list.) I offered my skirt for sale to the room at large. A green, alien-looking figure lay prone in mid-air, hovering at eye-level and apparently sleeping. Nightclub Man levitated well above the crowd, and boogied again. "Dancing on AIR!" he exclaimed.

It continued in this way for some time. I was mostly ignored, occasionally propositioned for text-based sex and wholly unable to conduct business. I am sad to report that peddling homegrown pixelbling to ultra-Goth Furries requires a skill set I do not have. Those who make money here are better sellers than I.

I spent another hour in-world, succeeding only in getting lost, cursed at and stuck in a vacant house. On my Yale-hardened weird-o-meter, literally everyone I encountered buried the needle.

Judging by my brief visit, Second Life has more in common with an AOL chat room than a digital economy. For all its promise of immersive neo-capitalist escapism, it seems a little too trivial, better in concept than in execution. (Admittedly, a similar verdict might emerge if we judged our entire culture by a single visit to an Anime convention.)

In-world, life goes on. Reuters now reports that Ginko Financial, the SL bank that pays 44 percent annual interest, is quite possibly a pyramid scheme. Between this and the nude dancers, Second Life has a certain rawness, like a gold-rush border town: all skin merchants and Ponzis, quick buck artists and land grabs; a Star Wars cantina in the digital realm.

Let's be frank. From what I saw, Second Life is a nerdy, Jolt-fueled pastime for social cripples and perverts. It may yet do well, but like myriad frontier outposts before it - and of course, the Internet itself - it will start out sketchy before the bland hordes move in.

MISCELLANY

WHERE DID ALL THE DINOSAURS GO?

OCTOBER 6, 2004

Walk around Yale these days and you're likely to find signs for the "Success by Six" campaign. I've spotted them throughout the campus, hawking an admirable program urging adults to pay attention to children during the formative early years of their life. A noble goal, one permitting some richly deserved reflection on the disappointments of adulthood.

Among the myriad pleasures of being a grown-up, certain bitter pills do exist. Sure, it's terrific to smoke, vote, drink and drive -- though hopefully not in that order -- but some features of maturity are, being fair, downright disappointing.

Consider dinosaurs. If your childhood mirrored mine in even the broadest sense, you were inundated from an early age with these colossal brutes. Stories of their massive frames and carnivorous antics buoyed your early imagination. You studied them in grade school, drew pictures of them, saw them constantly on television, in books, advertisements. Dinosaurs were a pillar of childhood, as pervasive as traffic. And where are they now?

Speaking only for myself, I always assumed a certain portability of knowledge when it came to classroom subjects. Consciously or not, the notion did exist that I was attending school to learn things relevant to my future life. This belief is, I think, fairly common, and a child could rightly express dismay if, for instance, he struggled through years of decimal arithmetic only to discover that adults favored working their sums in binary.

This was exactly the smart of injustice I felt -- dampened only slightly by years of collegiate education -- when dinosaurs came up in recent conversation. With a rush of memory, all manner of facts came tumbling back -- the Diplodocus, I said, had a second brain in its tail! The Stegosaurus used its formidable spines for heat exchange as well as defense! At once, I remembered an avalanche of dinosaur books, videos, fourth-grade discussions, and I distinctly recalled engaging, with an optimism so naive in hindsight, in rote memorization of the names, classes and characteristics of these beasts. Surely, this would stand me in good stead later on?

Hardly. A significant feature of early childhood, dinosaurs are notably absent from our daily lives today. We've moved on, enamored now with autos, clothing and elections. And while these are undoubtedly relevant -- elections in particular must be monitored with extreme caution, as November 2000 amply demonstrated -- I object to the sidelining of our antique, leathery friends. Would it really be so hard to bring dinosaurs back into the mix? Why not open some dino-themed gas stations? Play a round of Dinosaur Monopoly? Or perhaps we should institute some creative branding, mirroring that which once flooded us on morning television. I might not drive a Ford Iguanodon, but I certainly wouldn't fault the fellow who did.

In keeping with the priorities we internalized as kids, The New York Times should devote at least one full section to meandering discussion of dinosaur anecdotes, heavily laden with "artist's conceptions" and epic illustrations of nature's justice cruelly meted out in the primitive food chain. Why not quarry the vast Latin tableau of dinosaur names for our children themselves? A quick glance at the Social Security Administration's online list of the top thousand baby names should quell any uncertainty you may harbor regarding the suitability of "Allosaur" as a kid's handle; with 270 girls named "Lexus" last year alone -- and "Armani" cruelly applied to 265 unwitting boys -- the market is clearly ripe for new monikers.

Dinosaurs aren't the only omnipresent feature of childhood gone mysteriously AWOL, though they are perhaps one of the more universal. Other time-bombs of juvenile disappointment abound: Consider the sad day when a child realizes that ghosts are of virtually no interest to your average grown-up, or indeed, that the concept of a "grown-up" doesn't even exist past puberty. And let's not even get into the fact that many of the dinosaurs we adored as children turn out never to have existed -- a rude revelation on par with my stunning discovery that, following the Apollo missions, man never returned to the moon. "You mean we just left that moon rover up there?" No Flintstones vitamins were eaten on that day, so deep was my disenchantment with mankind.

We're setting our kids up for some nasty falls, pumping them full of spurious material and skewed priorities in preparation for some wholly imagined future they'll never inherit. Let's face the facts: Adults never really liked dinosaurs -- they feigned interest to make us like them. Dinosaurs, like ghosts, lunar missions and unsolved mysteries, offer incalculable benefits to the hurried adult, permitting children to immerse themselves in richly entertaining material with no bearing on the real world. Children rely on adults for guidance, and we submerge them in trivialities. This cries out for reform -- but far from striking dinosaurs from the juvenile curriculum, let's attack the injustice from the other end, and bring those monsters back into play.

Architects of "Success by Six," heed this clarion call: We owe it to tomorrow's 6-year-olds to forge a world they'll be glad to live in. And just so we're clear, this means more ghosts, more dinosaurs and fresh kudos to SpaceShipOne.

YALIES MUST EMBRACE LOVE'S RANDOM NATURE

FEBRUARY 16, 2006

Setting the stage for Sex Week at Yale, last Friday's scene section featured an article that claimed Yalies are too busy for relationships ("My so-called sex life," 2/10). It seems between class, sports, work and extracurricular activities, our overachieving undergraduates have no time for the luxury of human pair-bonding. I suspect St. Valentine would be deeply troubled by this romance deficit. So, in hopes of shaking some trees or jumping some motors, I offer what absolutely no one has asked for: my take on our troubles with love.

Let's start simple. Sex is vital to human existence. Pair-bonding and the strangely taboo activities that stem from it are all that really matter to our species. Everyone alive today is blessed with a stellar pedigree -- we are the progeny of Those Who Got It On, a staggering lineage of sexually-active survivors that stretches unbroken to the dawn of man. I shouldn't have to tell you this, but those hirsute hunks didn't scratch out a living in dank caves or battle saber-toothed tigers so you could favor IM squash over getting laid. Smarten up, kids.

But it's not that straightforward. In the survey that accompanied Friday's article, most students confessed to getting jiggy within the past seven days. It's not sex Yalies are passing on, it's dating.

Here we differ from our distant ancestor, who shivered beneath the stars and swung a spiked club. For him, courtship and coitus were fairly clear-cut -- one begat the other, and mate choice had real meaning.

We hook up casually, but scrutinize potential boyfriends with a jeweler's eye. We sample fertile girlfriends yet produce no babies. Our courtship ritual is detached from its ultimate goal. If students readily engage in sex but postpone serious efforts at mate choice, then the cart has come before the biological horse.

Why are we such picky daters? I blame the pervasive and resilient fiction that one ideal mate exists for each and every person. Whereas choosing a partner capable of basic sexual function is not especially challenging (unless it's last call at Toad's), choosing a boyfriend or girlfriend has become far more difficult. A daunting array of emotional, intellectual and chemical factors must mesh before we anoint our mate. And for that final walk down the aisle, gosh, everything better be thrice-checked and mission-perfect. Someone call NASA.

Jerry Seinfeld famously parodied skittish lovers who scuttle relationships over trifles. Drunk on options, they skip between dates, chasing some elusive vision of perfection. And today, who can blame them? A guy can log onto the Internet, and within five clicks be chatting with singles overseas. Girls know jostling hordes wait to beg their digits at any bar. Why stick around when there's a better date just over that hill? Why settle when somewhere, your one true love awaits?

I'll tell you why. The lock-and-key notion that one single star-fated love-match exists for every human couldn't possibly be true. If we were that fussy about mating, procreation would be a combinatorial nightmare; we'd never have made it this far. We could each be happy with many different people, only a small subset of whom we'll ever encounter.

But the Internet is changing that. We are no longer restricted to screening dates in our school, our town, even our country. Just imagine how many ideal mates lurk among the six billion souls trudging this planet ? and some aren't even online yet. Literally any day, your perfect match could log on, post a pixellated siren-song and dash your life to pieces. It's enough to give even the most committed lover pause.

For an interesting twist on this, consider ABC's "The Bachelor." On this program, 25 nubile ladies vie for the affections of one well-heeled dreamboat. This fellow engages in a massively-parallel flurry of zero-sum romance, paring down his gaggle of hopefuls until one remains. Whatever drama awaits in the elimination, one thing is for certain: the winner is always there -- she has been standing in that crowd since day one. The game is a closed system, and no rum-fuelled hookups can upset the ritual. Juxtaposed with the frenzied horizon-gazing of real-world dating, this arrangement is strangely calming. If only life were so phony.

Back to reality. What's a Yalie to do? Internet dating is for dorks, "The Bachelor" is profligate escapism, and you're not too selective -- you're just busy, right?

Fine. But if you ever finish that problem set and decide to hunt for mates, remember: Countless people could make you happy, if you'd just commit to one. There's no such thing as the perfect match.

And if the thought of settling terrifies you, it really needn't. Biology saves the day. Love is a complex emotional and neurochemical cocktail, a feeling that says, "logic and statistics be damned, I have found my one ideal match." And true or not, it's the closest thing to transcending mundane reality in the entire human experience. It's even better than a cappella.

So stop warming the bench, Yale. Close the books tonight. Make a caveman proud.

ROAD RALLIES: NOT JUST FOR MILLIONAIRES ANYMORE

JANUARY 19, 2006

Imagine tearing up the freeway in an Italian V-12, dodging speed traps and blasting flat-out to a checkpoint. Imagine outrunning carjacking gangs in Latvia, or streaking across Morocco with the King's permission to speed with impunity. Now picture doing this with 300 crazy rich people, and you have some inkling of what happens every year on the Gumball 3000.

If you can't manage the four-figure speeding fines, five-figure entry fees or six-figure cars of the Gumball 3000, other rallies offer excitement at a fraction the cost. Whatever their stripe or target demographic, road rallies are really marvelous fun.

I was hooked from age four, when I first watched that black Lamborghini tear up the opening credits in "Cannonball Run." This popular comedy was based on a real event: The Cannonball Baker Memorial Sea-to-Shining-Sea Trophy Dash.

The Cannonball was an underground cross-country road race: a no-rules, non-stop outlaw sprint from New York to Los Angeles that fast became an automotive legend. In 1971, racing legend Dan Gurney won in a Ferrari Daytona, hitting speeds in excess of 170 mph and finishing the 2,900-mile drive in less than 36 hours. One rival team answered a classified ad, and agreed to transport a Cadillac Sedan de Ville across the country for a wealthy businessman; they did so in just 37 hours, and were only narrowly beaten to the finish by a customized van laden with 350 gallons of fuel. The Cannonball was run only five times, but spawned a rash of movies and remains firmly rooted in the annals of automotive history.

It was not until 1999 that an event rivaled the notoriety of the Cannonball, when British millionaire Maximillion Cooper invited 50 friends on a 3,000-mile jaunt around Europe. His event spanned six days, with planned stops for wild parties at five-star hotels. No official time was kept, and no prizes were awarded for placement. Instead, competitors roared across the continent in million-dollar cars plastered with sponsor decals, partied like the Rolling Stones and left stunned onlookers in their wake. The Gumball 3000 was born.

Since then, the Gumball has become a massive affair. Hundreds of supercars participate in this annual orgy of speed, and several TV specials, films and magazine features have followed it. Our overspending, MTV-fed society devours so-called "aspirational lifestyle events" with a special ferocity, and this all-out, blinged-up brand of fast-living delinquency definitely fits the bill. The Gumball has spawned more copycat events than can comfortably be listed here; but whatever their distinct slant, they all share a common theme: a gaggle of teams drive long distances, party hard and generally live it up. To the dismay of lawmen and the delight of county treasurers, cross-country rallying has once again gone mainstream.

Defending such rallies is a delicate task, since no legally satisfying justification exists for speeding around on public highways, however exciting it may be. Maximillion's official angle is that the Gumball

3000 does not sanction breaking the law; and although his edict is often delivered to raucous laughter and a good number of nudges, he maintains a poker face and the story nonetheless stands. Most major rallies exist in this gray area: They officially prohibit speeding, but some participants do so anyway.

Opponents argue that a driver speeding in a Ferrari -- no matter how competent -- will compromise public safety; but despite six years and almost 20,000 miles covered by hundreds of supercars at outrageous speeds, not one fatal crash has occurred on the Gumball 3000. Personally, I worry more about road users applying makeup while barking into a cell phone and dressing kids in the passenger seat, or weaving along in the fast lane with no idea how their 5,000-lb. SUV behaves in the wet. Speed may aggravate matters, but a good number of people probably shouldn't be driving at any pace. Inattention and complacency breed highway hazard.

Of course, this debate becomes moot when all participants obey posted speed laws. I've done several rallies myself, and can assure you that tremendous fun can be had whilst obeying the legal limit. (Indeed, the famed Cannonballers of old discovered that driving near the speed limit often won the race; the Cadillac that averaged almost 100 mph lost far too much time to traffic stops.)

A good rally is not a speed race, and not quite a road trip; it's sort of an anything-goes party on wheels, an amalgamation of cars, good friends and zany competition. The great rallies succeed in fusing the Cannonball's daring with the wacky cheer of the ensuing films and the decadent joie de vivre of the Gumball 3000 -- no small feat for a bunch of yahoos driving student cars up I-95.

You don't need a Carrera GT to have a great time on the road. Join an established group, or gather some friends and seed your own event. Mind the speed limit, and you'll have a terrific time.

TRIANGLE MYSTERY DOESN'T STAND UP TO SCRUTINY

JANUARY 25, 2007

As I begin my final semester of graduate school, I must report a troubling discovery: Throughout my many years of post-secondary education, I have never once questioned the myth of the Bermuda Triangle.

I realized this last week, when a TV announcer mentioned the legend. Those two words conjured countless youthful hours spent enthralled by fantastic tales of vanishing planes, missing ships and mariners lost without a trace. As a child, I accepted the Triangle as de facto reality; this belief somehow survived more than two decades of schooling and left me subliminally freighted with a secret thirst for mysterious mishaps in the mid-Atlantic.

The young mind is particularly hospitable to fantasy, and tall tales of paranormal activity, in my estimation, serve chiefly to occupy children on long car-rides. In this regard, the Bermuda Triangle certainly worked on me.

Oh, how I loved that mysterious plot of sea. How thrilling it was, how invigorating, to drink the nectar of its tales, to stand at the precipice of the unknown and cast a timid gaze into that abyss. To think: an infamous patch of water where compasses failed, freak tornados swallowed Cessnas, and unexplained phenomena gobbled unsuspecting sailors. Pure fourth-grade catnip.

In my case, this relic had outlived its usefulness around the time of M.C. Hammer. But somehow it has persisted, long past parachute pants and Pogo Balls.

The time has come finally to debunk the myth. Irrational fascination with scary shapes of sea simply shall not stand.

I'll keep this brief: a swift blast of fresh air through the musty corridors of the mind. Armed with years, skepticism — and better still, the Internet — let us revisit the Bermuda Triangle.

First, some general knowledge: The infamous triangle is actually a huge body of water. It spans a busy shipping lane, and commercial airplanes pass through it virtually nonstop. And when did the news last report a jetliner gone missing in the Bermuda Triangle? If some strange risk does exist there, it must be almost imperceptibly small. Strike one for the myth.

Digging a little, we find that Lloyd's of London, the international insurance market, does not recognize the triangle as unusual and charges no premium for traversing it. Now, however skittish I may be about sea-monsters and magnetic storms, I grant that insurance men are at least doubly so. If it's all right by them, it's all right by me. A solid strike two.

Next, we seek the source of the legend.

The myth appears to stem from only a handful of disappearances. Chief among these is the mystery of Flight 19, a squadron of Navy planes that vanished off the coast of Florida in 1945. As the story goes, this group of seasoned aviators experienced strange compass malfunctions, radioed for help, and promptly vanished on a clear summer day. This account omits, however, that only lead pilot Charles Taylor had significant flying experience — and he allegedly had a history of getting lost while airborne, having ditched twice in the Pacific for this reason. In radio conversations during the ill-fated foray (which in fact lasted several hours) he appeared disoriented and completely lost; by the time of his final transmission, the planes were low on fuel and nowhere near land, and bad weather had arrived. Unfortunate? Sure. Inexplicable? Not so much.

The Navy's initial report blamed Taylor's confusion for the squadron's disappearance, but at the request of his family this was later changed to "cause unknown." It was apparently this report, combined with the 1948 disappearance of an airliner nearby, that gave rise to the myth.

While any region can play host to unexplained disappearances, the loss rate in the triangle is in line with expectation. Further, most staples of triangle lore lend themselves, in fact, to fairly ho-hum explanations. Strike three.

With that, I feel we have sufficiently aerated the myth of the Bermuda Triangle. Any who choose still to endorse it can begin by refuting these points.

I did learn some interesting things along the way. For instance, the Bermuda Triangle is a much more recent construction than I first assumed. The earliest recorded mention of anything resembling the modern myth came in a 1950 newspaper article, and the term itself was not coined until 1964. This is unexpected, given the abundance of far older shipwrecks now attributed to it.

It also shares a Yale connection. The late Charles Berlitz '36, polyglot and heir to the eponymous language empire, authored an utterly sensationalist expose titled "The Bermuda Triangle" in 1974, in which he posited time travel, dimensional portals, alien abduction and Atlantis as possible explanations for disappearing craft. This book — in all its wildly embellished, Bigfoot-citing glory — sold over 20 million copies and is widely credited with seeding public fascination with the triangle.

Sure, the Bermuda Triangle is just a few unsolved disappearances blown way out of proportion: a scaffold onto which years of supernatural hyperbole is draped. But if a magna cum laude Yalie who spoke 32 languages and wrote about Roswell says Bigfoot is to blame, really, who are we to argue?

WHEN DILIGENT PURITANS GET LAZY, WE GET 'NEW ENGLAND'

OCTOBER 19, 2004

Columbus Day always seems to spur a fair amount of dining-hall debate on the broad issues of imperialism, colonialism and western influence foisted upon poor benighted natives. But despite this chatter, it's the trivial aspects of North American settlement that unfailingly command my interest. Like the fact that the bulk of place names in New England are either thinly veiled modifications, or shamelessly copped duplicates, of some British equivalent.

Let's think about this. After the initial discovery of the New World -- and after Amerigo Vespucci's classic cartographic coup de grace slyly renamed an entire continent -- the settlers arrived. Whether escaping Old World persecution or wagering on new fortunes, they absconded, leaving creativity behind: Colonizing these shores, they named virtually every village after an established British town.

Now I grant, the founding fathers sometimes had the presence of mind to attach the prefix "New" to their place names. With this handy solution, those charged with christening a fledgling township could cobble together a unique name without taxing the imagination. In this manner, London became New London and so on, and true to form, the entire region was dubbed New England. But for people so disenchanted with Britain that they were driven to emigrate -- people whose flight to America is the stuff of legend, people who would later repulse British rule altogether -- such unabashed affection for king and country is unexpected.

I'm surprised by this lack of imagination. As a current-day corollary, imagine we get our act together, assemble a Mars mission and send astronauts to tame the red planet. Despite a strong affinity for the city of my birth, I would nonetheless be deeply dismayed if these trailblazing colonists named their outpost New Toronto. Besides being unoriginal in the extreme, this practice debases the spirit of exploration and threatens serious confusion. Meet my friend, just arrived from New-New-Haven. "Wait, do you mean New Haven, or New-New-Haven -- you know, the one on Mars?"

I suppose the Puritans were, to an extent, unwilling pioneers -- a morbid fear of state religion doesn't commonly fuel modern arctic explorers or astronauts, for instance -- but this does little to excuse their banal naming conventions. Some folks landed in America, struck camp and after three sober cheers for successful elusion of the Church of England, sat down to name their town. "Hey," cried Brother John, "I've got an idea -- let's name it after the place we just left!" No, hold on, you mean the one where they persecuted us? The one we fled? Yeah, that's the one.

And this didn't happen once, or twice; it happened every time. Plymouth? Ripped off. Southport? Milford? Boosted. Danbury, Brighton, Cambridge? Stolen. Stratford? Some of these names are so hot, they could fry an egg. Fleeing London? Welcome to New London. Just left York? You'll surely enjoy New York. (Though to be fair, New York was originally New Amsterdam; the Dutch were evidently no more creative.)

Whatever the cause, our local place names are a bricolage of words culled from British maps, occasionally prefixed or saddled with compass points. Haven is taken, you say? Fine, we'll go with New Haven, North Haven, West Haven and East Haven. Sure looks nice up that way -- let's call that Fair Haven.

It really need not have been this way. Some parts of New England and Cape Cod sport the most delightful names, like Woonsocket, Narragansett and Wickaboxet. Town names in Pennsylvania charm with their stochastic, evocative tone: During a recent furlough, I passed Blue Ball, Intercourse, Bird-in-Hand and Pillow, all in the space of an afternoon. Hats off to the Keystone State! That so many settlers evidently got it right should compel even a staunch traditionalist to slam these much-lauded Puritans.

Still, as you have by now undoubtedly surmised, I am neither a historian nor particularly versed in 17th-century history; a general grasp of the Mayflower Compact is basically the summit of my early colonial knowledge. Nonetheless, I refuse to accept that cooking up an interesting name or two was beyond even the most stoic Puritan colonist. Relevant, catchy words abound in the colonial lexicon: Plough, harvest and pumpkin could easily be pressed into service as town names. At the very least, they could have used "Not" instead of "New" to prefix their names. After all, Not York, Not London and Not England are just as snappy, and if you ask me, far more informative.

REMEMBERING A FRIEND, WILLIAM F. BUCKLEY JR.

FEBRUARY 28, 2008

I first met Bill Buckley five years ago, after responding to an advertisement he published in the News. The ad was small, buried in the leaves of the campus daily. Beneath a soaring seabird were written the words, "Do you like to sail?"

Buckley, a famous political figure and author, was a legendary sailor — and back then, he was looking for a first mate to accompany him aboard his sloop Patito as he sailed on Long Island Sound. Unlike the hordes of blazer-clad conservative youth who would no doubt trade significant hardship for an audience with their hero, my only real exposure to Mr. Buckley had come from watching a DVD archive of his 1969 Firing Line debate with Noam Chomsky.

Despite this evident handicap, he invited me for an interview over lunch. I vowed to do Noam proud.

After bloody Marys and a few glasses of wine, I remember feeling somewhat surreal, like I was a guest on his long-running program. I was having a swell time, but tried not to get too comfortable — since I was convinced that as soon as he found out I opposed the imminent Iraq invasion, our pleasant repartee would dry up. Deep into the meal and no doubt emboldened by drink, I broached the subject. There ensued a lively and quite heated discussion, at the end of which he hired me to sail with him.

That first lunch was the only time we really talked politics. I had thought it important to mark my ground, to make clear that I wasn't about to discard my convictions (youthful as they were) just to land a sailing gig. But more significant was what I learned about Bill: He didn't let politics dictate his friendships. Though famous for his conservative thought, he not only held court with avowed liberals, but charmed them utterly, too.

We sailed weekly in the sound that summer. Sailing with Bill Buckley was unlike anything I'd seen before, or since. The entire galley storage aboard Patito was routinely commandeered with the makings of just one lavish dinner; condiments occupied the whole starboard cupboard. We relaxed and talked with his guests, ate scandalously well and, just once, ran aground (hard!) in Stamford harbor. Bill's absolute arsenal of $10 words made him not only a famously eloquent speaker but a potent adversary at the word game 'ghost,' which, perhaps not coincidentally, he always had us play. His mischievous smile and unflagging joie de vivre made those trips unforgettable.

Buckley the writer was equally remarkable. He wrote, in addition to his regular syndicated column, a full-length book every year; this he generally banged out all at once during a few short weeks abroad.

In spring 2005, I accompanied Bill and his wife Pat to the Bahamas to help work on what would be his last novel, "The Rake." Our routine was set: We worked in the morning, broke for lunch, then took our daily walk around Lyford Cay to discuss the characters, the story and life in general. Watching a book take shape a few thousand words at a time dashed my conceptions of how a novel is written (and how long it takes) and spurred me to start one myself — an endeavor which proceeded briskly in Nassau but wallowed in Connecticut. Sharing a desk in paradise with one of the sharpest and most prolific writers of our time is a creative catalyst not easily replaced.

Through days filled with music — for which I had lugged a 'portable' stereo to the Bahamas in an extra suitcase — and nights dining with Pat and the most captivating guests imaginable, Bill wrote swiftly and finished the book, on time of course. In a curious echo of the culinary largesse on the boat, he shipped an enormous suitcase to Nassau packed with reams and reams of heavy-bond paper and a full-size laser printer. When you wrote with Bill, the daily drafts were not just reviewed on-screen — they were printed 40 pages per minute on resume stock.

My time with Bill stands out for me as it might for anyone: a highlight and a rarity. Each day jammed full of work and play, of life lived as it should be. Bill Buckley lived like that every day. Over the years, I was privileged to join him from time to time, to ride alongside as he wrote, sailed, laughed and lived with his legendary intensity.

William F. Buckley, Jr. stood out, truly larger than life. Anyone I ever took to meet him came away enchanted. He was much to many — a legendary political figure, a beloved author, a magnanimous gentleman — and to this Yale student, ultimately, a great friend.

Columns by Publication Date

2004

2005

2005 CONTINUED

2006

2006 CONTINUED

2007

2008

www.ingramcontent.com/pod-product-compliance
Lightning Source LLC
LaVergne TN
LVHW011230080426
835509LV00005B/408